Va
The Messeng

*The story of a lost four-week-old kitten
who found his way from a
Greek Island to the British Isles.*

Derek Allen

Copyright © 2025 Derek Allen

All rights reserved. No part of this book may be reproduced
or used in any manner without the prior written
permission of the copyright owner.

This publication is registered with
Copyright House
World IP Registration House Ltd,
150 Minories, London, EC3N 1LS, UK

To Yana

x

Introduction - 7

Chapter One - 9
When will this nightmare ever end?

Chapter Two - 33
Fears and frustrations, genetic mutations,
locked down nations and novel vaccinations

Chapter Three - 60
First three weeks in Greece

Chapter Four - 93
Evia

Chapter Five - 126
The road to Krioneri

Chapter Six - 148
Return to Evia

Chapter Seven - 171
Prespas revisited

Chapter Eight - 197
The Road Home

Epilogue/Επίλογος - 224

Introduction

It's often said that things happen for a reason or something was meant to be. These popular sayings suggest that all events and experiences in our lives, whether positive or not, have a purpose or an underlying intention.

The Greek philosopher Aristotle is thought to have first coined the phrase *"everything happens for a purpose."* He believed that every person we meet and every experience we encounter is designed to help shape and form us into becoming the most excellent versions of ourselves. That the purpose of everything in nature, from the stars and planets to abandoned little kittens, was created to serve some function in our lives. The belief that things happen for a reason belongs to the realm of metaphysics, or μεταφυσική, it's a Greek word!

Meta: beyond, fysikí: natural, or beyond the natural. Scientists seek to create explanations for everything, so they tend to scoff at this particular philosophy.

To suggest that fate or destiny can determine or influence our lives is utterly irreconcilable with science. With science, everything has a cause. But not a reason.

Now, I'm not sure about any of this either. But one thing I am entirely sure about is that breaking away from daily routines and comfort zones, throwing caution to the wind, and setting off on a long road trip in a camper van nearly always leads to weird and wonderful things happening along the way.

And the destination shouldn't always be the purpose of a journey because the journey is, in itself, where everything happens...... for a reason.... or not.

Chapter One

When will this nightmare ever end?

By the beginning of January 2021, the whole country, and the rest of the planet, was in dire need of a booster to increase endorphin levels. Even wishing a Happy New Year to anyone was accompanied by a roll of the eyes and a follow-up*: "Let's hope it's a better one than last year."*

Only five days before Christmas, a new lockdown was imposed on the population of London and the southeast of England. Termed Tier 4, it effectively cancelled Christmas for nearly 18 million people or about a third of the population of England. The rest of the nation didn't escape unpunished either. Legally enforceable restrictions cancelled all seasonal jollies, and there was a stay-at-home order and a three-household limit on Christmas day get-togethers. Things were looking very bleak again.

Thus, UK Prime Minister Boris Johnson's festive bubble plan was burst by a new mutant variant of concern. This variant would be colloquially dubbed the Grinch variant for banjaxing the merriment of Christmas. While insisting there was no alternative, Boris Johnson announced, from his £2.6m briefing room, *"It is with a very heavy heart that I must tell you we cannot continue with Christmas as planned."* He went further by stating, *"We must be guided by the science."*

Little did the rest of us know, at the time, that Number 10 Downing Street was also being guided by copious bottles of Sauvignon Blanc and Pinot accompanied by the finest French fromage whilst dancing to Abba's greatest hits, all dished up during lockdown flouting parties and wine time Fridays. Although most of the population followed the public health rules of social distancing, mask-wearing, and singing Happy Birthday twice while washing hands, at the heart of government, they were all getting totally plastered.

It's also worth mentioning that illegal raves and large gatherings carried a maximum fine of £10,000. Busting the regulations, the rules on leaving the home, restrictions on small gatherings, etc, could also land you a fine between £200 and £6,400, depending on the severity of the offence.

Boris Johnson, his wife Carrie, and the UK Chancellor of the Exchequer, Rishi Sunak, were all issued with £100 fixed-penalty notices after it was concluded that they had all partied, along with up to 30 others, at a birthday bash. (£100 is 0.1% of £10,000…….. just saying.)

"COVID loves a crowd." declared government officials as the annual New Year's Eve fireworks display in London and all public gatherings were cancelled. Household mixing was banned indoors across England, while Wales, Scotland, and Northern Ireland were already in full-blown national lockdowns. Following concerns that the Tier 4 stay-at-home system was failing to contain the spread of the Alpha variant, the UK government imposed a third national lockdown on January 6th, 2021. Just 12 days later, on January 18th, it suspended all travel corridors to the UK. This meant that all international arrivals would be required to take a pre-departure COVID test and self-isolate immediately upon arrival for 10 days.

I think it's fair to say that by early to mid-January 2021, pandemic fatigue was taking a significant toll on the mental health of millions of people. Stress, isolation, loneliness, burnout, worry, anxiety, and depression all were reaching a breaking point that was just as harmful, if not worse, than the fear of catching the virus itself. When would the nightmare ever end?

****

Meanwhile, in the Middle of the Irish Sea

The Isle of Man is a self-governing British Crown Dependency slap bang in the middle of the Irish Sea. It's home to approximately 85,000 people, including me and my soul mate Claire. The island is 33 miles long by 13 miles wide. With a long, rugged coastline, stunning cliff-top views, sandy beaches, medieval castles, and a mountainous interior, the Isle of Man is a top contender for one of the most picturesque corners of the British Isles.

On March 26th 2020, in response to the COVID-19 pandemic, the government of the Isle of Man attempted to hermetically seal the island off. Except for freight and key workers, the borders and ports were all shut, and no new arrivals were permitted. Everyone was also required to stay at home, except for limited reasons, along with a raft of other measures designed to protect the community.

The island, like just about everywhere else, was in lockdown. Our full-time occupation as a music duo was among the first jobs to flatline as pubs, clubs, restaurants, entertainment venues, and hospitality venues all shut down. Our immediate dates and bookings were cancelled, and future bookings were thrown into doubt. But, all things considered, being locked down on a picturesque island with a rugged coastline and stunning cliff-top views didn't seem as harsh as some other locations around the world. As I recall, the local weather during April and May 2020 was primarily dry, with blue skies and sunshine. So we booted up and went hiking as often as we wanted along that rugged coastline.

When our local grocery store went into meltdown due to staff shortages, we happily signed up for shelf stacking duties, providing a temporary income and taking our minds off all the uncertainties whirling around. The Isle of Man government was also very prompt in offering various financial support measures for businesses and the self-employed. Nevertheless, as the days turned to weeks and dried pasta, tinned tomatoes, and toilet paper vanished from supermarket shelves, anxieties across the nation started to mount. Around this time, when mini bottles of hand sanitiser and antibacterial gels almost became black market currency, most of us realised this would not be short-term. We were all staring down the double barrels of an uncertain future. And it wasn't just pasta and toilet paper that were vanishing fast. Any thoughts of travelling anywhere were, at best, wishful thinking and, at worst, downright delusional.

Many strange and interesting new words, acronyms, and expressions emerged during the New Normal:

"Key workers, operating outside of their support bubbles, wearing PPE, but not self-isolating must socially distance to prevent community spread and help flatten the curve as the viral load of an asymptomatic carrier can risk a potential transmission, following an incubation period, if undetected by a track and trace threshold boundary to reduce false positives."

Overnight, everyone became familiar with the function of Polymerase Chain Reaction tests (abbreviated: PCR tests) and the differences between an immunocompromised and an immunosuppressed system. An extraordinary number of un-credited experts and wizards also emerged, willing to share their untrammelled knowledge of biology, epidemiology, pathology, virology, immunology, and all aspects of public health with anyone who would listen. Tik-Tok dance routines featuring nurses and doctors went viral after being uploaded to various online platforms. At the same time, our local postman could explain, in fine detail, the myriad differences and benefits between the N95 disposable face mask and the regular blue single-use surgical variety. It was a truly phenomenal period, albeit barking mad at times.

Towards the end of April 2020, trades like building and landscape gardening were allowed to return to work in the Isle of Man. Then, shortly after that, garden centres reopened along with some non-essential shops. By the middle of June, restaurants, pubs, and cafés were permitted to reopen, but only if they could offer a seated dining service. Then, towards the end of the month, life was practically back to normal within the Manx Bubble, the local colloquialism for the island's isolation from the rest of the planet.

On June 26th, we played our first gig in over three months at a local pub. It was a packed evening, full of revellers celebrating a return to normality for the first time in what seemed an eternity. I remember we kicked the night off by playing Queen's *Another One Bites The Dust.* It was intended as a veiled digitus impudicus, or middle finger, to COVID-19, lockdowns and the misery it brought to everyone. In hindsight, it was perhaps a tad premature to assume it was all over.

In early July, a government announcement was literally music to our ears. From July 20th, island residents would be permitted to travel to the UK and return without the journey being deemed essential travel. A travel declaration form, signed and delivered, would be required for the return journey, along with 14 days of isolation at home. But we considered that a small sacrifice to pay for the freedom to travel again.

However, we couldn't leave home immediately. We already had gigs booked on the 23rd of the month, playing on top of the Civic Centre roof in Castletown, south of the island, and a Marquee event on the 25th. But by the very next day, after the Marquee event, we were all packed and ready and on the ferry sailing from the Isle of Man to the Port of Heysham in Lancashire. We were back on the road again, in our trusty camper van, and the planned destination was Greece, just like the previous year, the year before, and every other year during the past decade.

On board the ferry, there was a notable dearth of other passengers. It's true that, for many people, it was still too early and too uncertain to make journeys greater than a trip to the local grocery store. Whether justified or not, the media and governments worldwide played a big part in fear-mongering.

I kept a diary at the time along with our online Facebook travel page, Rocking Life on the Road. The day before we left, I wrote: *"Back home, they think we are either very brave or very foolish to travel anywhere amid a worldwide pandemic."*

However, we fully intended to proceed cautiously on our journey and not allow irrational fears to thwart our plans. We did receive a couple of nasty comments during the early start of the trip, labelling us reckless super-spreaders. But to most others, we were like canaries down a coal mine or human guinea pigs. Messages followed us wherever we went, with questions about any restrictions encountered whilst travelling or any other out of the ordinary rules or regulations. After a quick visit to see Claire's family in Liverpool, we headed south to the English Channel coast. Even on the motorways, the traffic wasn't the usual full-on congestion. People were still very apprehensive about travelling.

In Dover, we boarded a ferry to Dunkirk without any hassles whatsoever, and upon arrival in France, we proceeded eastbound to Belgium. The year before, while travelling through southern Croatia, we met two German girls also travelling in a camper van. It was one of those chance meetings with two other like-minded "kindred spirits" that quickly developed into an enduring friendship. After Croatia, we met them again in Albania and then, once more, in Greece. During the winter months, and especially during lockdown, we'd kept in regular contact, sharing and comparing our lockdown experiences, anxieties, and tales of woe. So, naturally, a big reunion had been planned with our lovely German girls, Tzeni & Juli, in Düsseldorf.

Before driving into Germany, we also wanted to buy some Belgian chocolates as a small gift for Tzeni and Juli, so we pulled off the motorway and found a supermarket in the suburbs of Liège. Unhitching a shopping trolley, we made our way towards the automatic entrance doors of the large store. At the entrance, the uniformed Health-Security-Staff ordered us to stop. It was forbidden to enter the supermarket together. We also had to sanitise our hands at the sanitation station and don a face mask. So Claire dutifully complied with the regulations, took the trolley and entered the store on her own. But I wanted to go in too. So, once she had cleared health and safety security control and was now inside, I proceeded forward to squirt a dollop of antibacterial gel onto my hands. *"Stop!"* yelled the health security. *"You must enter with a trolley."Can I not just take a basket?"* I asked. *"No, enter only with a trolley."*

With no explanation for why trolleys were safer than baskets, I returned to the trolley shelter, popped a euro into the slot, and unhitched one all for myself. Inside, there was definitely an air of uneasiness among all the shoppers. Social distancing was rigorously adhered to, and there was hardly a sound from anyone, only the shuffle of shoes and the squeak of trolley wheels on the floor. There was a compulsory one-way system in force within the supermarket, which all shoppers obediently adhered to. It reminded me of the "walking the wheel" scene from the 1978 movie Midnight Express, where every prisoner has to walk clockwise around a symbolic centre. Belgians must have still been in the vigilance phase or possibly the critical phase of lockdown. Either way, it all felt very oppressive indeed.

I spotted Claire with her trolley ahead of me in the aisle and manoeuvred my trolley as close as possible without busting the 1.5 metre Belgian social distancing measure or *les gestes barrières* as they called it. She was next to the légumes section studying a packet of cherry tomatoes. Trying to maintain a low profile whilst not raising my voice in the supermarket's muted and slightly fearful atmosphere, I attempted to get Claire's attention. *"Hklaire, Hklaire."* My faint murmurs through the face mask made me sound like someone with chronic nasal congestion. She turned to face me. *"Hkave hyou hseen heny hokholates?"* I whispered in my stifled hypo-nasal speech. *"Hkno"* she replied. *"Hokay, Hi'll ho han hkave ha hlook,"* I said and sped past her, turning into the next aisle.

We'd already attracted enough attention, as *Les deux étrangers,* on the way in and didn't want to ruffle any more feathers. In the confectionery section of the aisle, I couldn't see any actual presentation boxes of assorted Belgian chocolates. So I turned to Claire, who had caught up with me, and said, *"Hthis his ahwaste hof htime, hthere's hno hoxes hof hokholates."* In Claire's trolley was a single packet of cherry tomatoes. I looked down the aisle at the long queue of shoppers waiting at the checkouts, looked again at the cherry tomatoes, then turned to Claire and said, *"Whell, hgood hluck hwith hthat, Hi'm houtta here,"* then turned and pushed my empty trolley to find the exit.

However, the only way to exit this store was via the checkouts. And it was far too narrow to squeeze past the other shoppers, all queuing with trolleys and the 1.5 metre social distance separating them. How could we leave the place without buying something and joining a ridiculously long queue?

I thought about abandoning the trolley and leapfrogging over the automatic entry barrier. But that would have alerted the health security, and no doubt I would have been tackled, then wrestled to the ground, and detained as a possible pilferer. Also, I wanted to reclaim my one euro coin in the trolley handle slot. Claire appeared behind me, minus the cherry tomatoes, and whispered, *"Hkow skhall hwe hget hout hof here?"* Then, I spotted a large Service Client sign next to a booth sealed off with a large clear sheet of acrylic glass. Behind this protective screen sat a woman surveying the checkout tills. So we approached her waving our hands in the air and she clearly understood our predicament because she waved us on past and through the automatic exit doors. Outside, we returned the trolleys, reclaimed our coins, and climbed back into the camper. *"Don't say a word,"* I said to Claire, who hadn't said a word.

We drove back into the late afternoon traffic and headed toward the suburb's centre. I parked and went off on foot, searching for a specialist chocolate shop somewhere down the side streets. In a small cobble-stoned square, I spotted what I was looking for. A quaint chocolaterie with the name Leonidas displayed atop the entrance. One other customer was inside the shop as I opened the door, tinkling a bell above me.

"Mais non Messieur, je vous en prie d'attendre l'extérieur." The lady behind the counter was scowling whilst shooing me outside with the back of her hand, gesturing that I leave the shop and wait my turn. *"Et portez un masque s'il vous plaît, avant d'entrer,"* she growled, instructing me to put on a face mask before entering her shop. Eventually, I returned to the camper clutching a little decorative plastic bag containing a gift box of assorted Belgian chocolates that had set me back a whopping 25 euros.

The following morning, we left the camper stop we had found in Blegny, Belgium, and drove towards Düsseldorf via Aachen, arriving about lunchtime. The girls had sent us their address details earlier and included a visible sign at the entrance to their driveway. We had no idea what this visible sign might be, as they never told us. But they assured us that we would understand immediately upon seeing it.

As we approached a busy street and inched ever closer, we spotted the visible sign. It was a pair of blue shorts hanging from a gatepost. This was a humorous swipe at my OCD for the colour blue, especially with regard to what I wear. It had been an inside gag since we met up in 2019.

A narrow driveway off the main street took us into a large courtyard with lock-up units, sheltered parking areas, and several ground-floor studios. It was like a mini-commune. This property belonged to Stelios, Tzeni's Greek dad, who had lived in Germany most of his adult life. He had decorated the walls, down his driveway, with murals depicting typical Greek vistas. From the Parthenon of the Athenian Acropolis to the white-washed houses of the Cyclades islands, there was no mistaking the Hellenistic influence of Stelios. Even the front of his home looked like the entrance to a traditional Greek taverna with authentic rickety wooden chairs around several wooden tables. Rapid tremolo pickings of a Greek Bouzouki could also be heard in the background.

It was a beautiful sunny afternoon, and we all lazed outside in the shade on hammocks strung up along the back wall. I baked fruit scones for a typical English afternoon cream tea. I'd smuggled a tub of clotted cream from the UK just for the occasion.

That evening, Stelios invited everyone for pizza at an outdoor restaurant in the city. Tzeni and Juli had already planned a return trip to Greece in their van, departing in a week. So, over dinner, we decided we'd meet them there later in the month, and Stelios offered his help arranging our ferry tickets.

The following morning, he drove me to his favourite travel agent, in the Greek quarter of town, where I could book and pay for the tickets. It felt like I was in a suburb of Athens with the hustle and bustle on the streets, the stores and bakeries with Greek shop fronts and signage and the Greek language spoken everywhere. As we approached the travel agents, there were no parking spaces to be found, so Stelios flicked on the hazard lights, stepped out, and left his car double parked—Greek-style.

Inside, seated opposite a lady next to a computer screen, Stelios struck up an in-depth conversation about current affairs, lockdowns, the economy, politics, family, and the weather; he talked about everything, excluding the purchase of our ferry tickets. I kept glancing outside the window at his abandoned car, half expecting a police presence by now. But it remained double-parked and undisturbed and clearly wasn't bothering anyone.

Finally, we got around to shipping timetables and the availability of a ferry from Ancona, Italy, to the Greek port of Igoumenitsa on August 21st. This would allow us at least another ten days or so to explore some of Germany before heading south to Italy. After the travel agent had made several phone calls, it was all done and dusted. We were booked. But as soon as I had paid for the tickets and stepped back outside, a strange gut feeling crept over me, wiggling its way into my conscious mind. That feeling that nags at your better judgement and decision-making. A powerful inner perception that you ignore at your peril.

In the bright sunshine, we strolled a short distance to a bakery where Stelios purchased a large selection of sweet and savoury Greek pastries. We then returned to his place and enjoyed a late alfresco breakfast with Claire, Tzeni and Juli.

After breakfast, the weather was fantastic, so a snap decision was made to unhook the bikes and cycle along the River Rhine to the city centre. Tzeni led the way on her bicycle, and we soon found ourselves in the beautiful Altstadt or Düsseldorf's old town.

Later that afternoon, when we returned to the mini-commune, Stelios was planning a fantastic Greek feast for the evening. Long tables were set, and benches were arranged in the courtyard to accommodate friends and family. It was the perfect setting for an impromptu music event. So we took all our gear from the camper. That's the PA speaker system & mixer, guitar amp, microphones, guitar, mini-keyboard, cabling, etc, and set it all up in a corner of the yard. The courtyard actually offered excellent acoustics, and our sound was full and loud. The sound waves were also spilling over into the nearby community.

Live music is always an attention grabber, and after about three songs into our set, we noticed balcony doors and windows opening from the neighbouring apartment blocks. People were waving and dancing from verandas overlooking us. At that precise moment, I had the distinct feeling that any kind of fun or entertainment was most welcome here, following many months of lockdown and stay-at-home orders.

The following day, we had to say our farewells and get back on the road again. We had been booked to play a gig the following Sunday at an outdoor beer garden in the municipality of Bellenberg, Bavaria. The venue/pub *Die Traube* (The Grape) had booked us several times for live music in the past, and we were delighted to take up the challenge once again. It's a lively, rockin' biker pub with a great atmosphere and boasts the slogan "The bar too tough to die." Inside, you can literally smell the leather.

The day before our gig, we stopped at *Die Traube* to speak with the owner, a biker girl named Chrissie. I had brought a bottle of eight-year-old rich, robust and soul-stirring stuff from the Isle of Skye for her fine collection of Scottish single malt and blended whiskies. She was clearly very relieved to be back open for business following Germany's nationwide lockdown. Nevertheless, strict social-distancing regulations were still enforced everywhere, hence our gig outdoors in the beer garden. We asked when she wanted us to start playing the following evening, and she said, *"Oh, it's Frühschoppen, so please can you begin about 11:00?"*

"Früh-what-in?" I replied, followed by, *"Isn't 11:00 a bit too late in the evening to start the gig?" "Nein."* she answered. *"It's Frühschoppen; it's the first pint of the day on Sundays here in Bavaria, so please start playing around 11:00....in the morning."*

She also told us we were the first music act she had booked since lockdown restrictions had eased in Germany. In other words, she was expecting a good turnout for the gig. So the following morning, early, we lugged all our gear into the back of the pub, where there was a sizeable beer garden. It was decorated with sculptures of the Blues Brothers alongside posters of Rock gods such as Jimi Hendrix, AC/DC and Mick Jagger's lips next to retro wall art featuring Kentucky Bourbon and vintage motorcycles. There was even a covered stage area set on wooden pallets facing the neatly arranged long tables and benches. With all our equipment set up and sound checks completed, we waited for the official opening of Frühschoppen at *Die Traube*.

The place soon filled up with locals and bikers alike, and we spent the following 2 hours belting out the hits. Although dancing was banned under German COVID rules, shaking and swaying while seated at the table was permitted, and everyone seemed to enjoy themselves.

To buy beer from the outdoor bar, customers had to comply with the face covering rule, which didn't explicitly require wearing a face mask. So, all customers seeking refills pulled T-shirts over their mouth and noses and made their way to the beer taps. Back at the tables, T-shirts were re-adjusted, and beer was consumed with great gusto. It was apparent to everyone that none of these dictums made any sense whatsoever.

After our gig, we hung around for a few hours to chat with some of the *Frühschoppers* and sample a stein or three of *Hefeweizenschluckweissbier*. Chrissy also offered us a plate of *Bayerische Weißwurst mit süßem Senf und Brezel*. Bavarian white sausage served with sweet mustard and soft pretzel. It was delicious.

The next day, we were on our way to Memmingen, a beautiful historic Bavarian town with an Altstadt considered one of the best preserved in southern Germany. But before we left Bellenberg, I hesitantly glanced at the latest news reports from the UK. We knew the UK government had removed Spain from a travel corridor exemption list two weeks earlier. This basically meant that thousands of British tourists, already on holiday in Spain and the popular Balearic Islands, had to rush home before the deadline of 11:00 a.m. on July 26th to avoid 14 days of quarantine. The sudden news had left holidaymakers shocked, confused, and angry. In many cases, there simply wasn't enough capacity on planes, trains, and boats to transport the sheer numbers trying to get home in time.

The latest news that morning also reported that Belgium and Luxembourg had been added to the UK's Black List. This information nagged at us as we drove the short distance to Memmingen. It was starting to cast a dark shadow over our plans. If the UK government was shutting down travel corridors, it would certainly be conceivable that other countries would soon follow suit. And then what?

After parking at a camper stop in Memmingen, we got the bikes off and went for a long cycle ride through Bavaria's wonderful countryside and forest paths. If anything, just to clear our thoughts of travel corridors. Later that day, I sent messages to friends in Western Greece asking about their current situation. I also called my good buddy Nick in Athens for his perspective and thoughts on the ever-shifting sands of government policy. We were anxiously seeking advice, a second opinion or any suggestions for our own travel plans down to Greece in less than 10 days' time. Of course, that ever-elusive crystal ball was forever eluding us, but we knew that we'd have to decide soon, one way or another.

Then, a few days later, France and The Netherlands were added to the UK quarantine list. The gut feeling that had wiggled its way into my conscious mind back in Düsseldorf had turned out to be quite legitimate.

So, after hearing the troubling news about France and the Netherlands, we decided to abandon the plan to continue on to Greece. It wasn't a rash decision or borne out of irrational fear. If EU countries started imposing quarantines in line with the UK, or worse, shut their borders entirely, we could suddenly find ourselves stranded far, far from home. And that was hardly an acceptable prospect.

****

Public Health Passenger Locator Forms

By August 2020, I had been together with Claire for 19 years and married for 14 of them. And in all that time, I'd never known her to stress out or overly worry about anything. She could effortlessly put the Cool back into Snoopy's alter-ego, Joe.

However, in the early hours of September 17th, 2020, at a small camper stop in the village of Heimbach, located in the Eifel hills of North Rhine-Westphalia, all that was about to change dramatically.

It was around two in the morning when Claire sat bolt upright in bed, almost hyperventilating. She then began rocking back and forth whilst displaying the symptoms of stress and anxiety and what seemed like an underlying mental health disorder. What had triggered this sudden acute panic attack? It was what I would later jokingly refer to as *PLF Syndrome.*

The PLF wasn't a new militant armed group recently formed in the Middle East. It was a Public Health Passenger Locator Form recently formed by EU and UK governments. It was yet another consequence of the ever-invasive COVID-19 regulations being ushered in worldwide. That day, September 17th, would be the day we would leave Germany and return to the UK. In normal times and under normal conditions, this wouldn't have presented us with any problems whatsoever. But these were not normal times.

Travellers returning to the UK from Germany were exempt from 14 days of quarantine because Germany was still included on the UK's travel corridor list. However, Belgium and France were not on this list. Seven weeks later, Germany and Sweden would also be assessed as posing a heightened infection risk and summarily removed from the UK travel corridors.

As there was no direct ferry crossing to England from Germany, we were compelled to transit Belgium and the northernmost region of France to get to Calais and, from there, back to the UK. To make this journey, we had to complete an online Public Health Passenger Locator Form separately for Belgium and the UK. These had to be submitted 72 hours before arrival. A Quick Response code, or QR code, would then be sent to the registered email address for future scanning. In the case of Belgium, it was all a bit too vague, as we had read elsewhere that the PLF was not required for transit passengers staying no longer than 48 hours in Belgian territory. But we submitted one anyway.

Claire had taken on the task of completing the Federal Public Service Health PLF for Belgium and for the UK's Visas & Immigration while I made the coffees. We couldn't establish if France required a PLF, so that was filed under "wait and see." Completing these forms was, in itself, an exercise in stress management. Failure to comply or inadvertently mess up a declaration could lead to staggeringly hefty fines en route and at our destination.

To transit back to the UK, we would have to book ourselves onto the shuttle, the rail link through the Channel Tunnel, from Calais to Folkstone. This transport mode meant we could remain isolated inside the camper.

Furthermore, we were not permitted to exit the vehicle anywhere from our last stop in Germany until we reached England. After the sheer joy of six fabulous weeks in beautiful Germany, driving over 2,400 miles throughout the country and cycling over 700 miles of cycle paths, the self-imposed responsibility of the PLF form filling and red tape finally caused Claire to crack.

And so it came to pass that on September 17th, at 2:00 a.m., I had to comfort and console her and assure her that all would be fine, that she had completed the online forms correctly, and that we wouldn't get into any trouble.

Surreptitiously, I was also in meltdown, feeling just as rattled as Claire was and very apprehensive about the journey ahead. Anyway, we set off from Heimbach at precisely "08:00 hours" and drove the short distance to Monschau, a town on the German-Belgian border. We stopped there to tank up with diesel and buy a few provisions and snacks for the rest of the journey. We consciously kept all receipts for our purchases to prove that we had been in Germany that morning, just in case the UK immigration authorities asked. Then with great trepidation, we continued the last mile to the Belgian border. In my head, all I could hear was the theme music from the 1968 blockbuster movie "Where Eagles Dare."

No other traffic was on the road, and no soul could be seen anywhere. We knew we had crossed the border because we drove past a standard blue EU road sign encircled with yellow stars with the word "Belgien" in the middle.

This was the area of Belgium known as the East Cantons, where German is the spoken language. The theme music in my head faded as we continued down the N67, passing through the beautiful Hautes Fagnes Natural Park. The only traffic we encountered was a tractor pulling a muck spreader and, in the opposite direction, two sport cyclists clad in high-visibility riding apparel.

All that anxiety and apprehension emanating from PLF forms, QR codes, and sworn declarations had been for nothing. There were no roadside health inspections, mobile police checks, hovering helicopters overhead, or signs of Belgian Special Forces. And remember that this was in the same country where it was compulsory for a couple to push two trolleys, one after the other, to enter a supermarket to purchase chocolate. The theme music from "Where Eagles Dare" had completely stopped playing in my head as we continued peacefully and unhindered to the town of Eupen, where we joined the E40/42 motorway.

Our race across Belgium via Liège, Brussels, Ghent and onto the Belgian coast had begun. So rapid was our advance that my imagination wandered back to May 1940.

Our very own Blitz across Belgium was similar to the direction taken by Army Group B of the German Wehrmacht commanded by Generalfeldmarschall Fedor von Bock during the Battle of France in May 1940. Therefore, after we had swooped past Liège and on to Brussels, I insisted that Claire refer to me, henceforth, as Generalfeldmarschall Erich von Manstein, and I would address her as Generaloberst Heinz Guderian. Our camper had also become the 9th Panzer Division of the German Wehrmacht. Claire continued crocheting, ignoring my lesson on history from the Second World War.

Claire's passion for crochet began several years earlier when she sought a new hobby to help her while away the hours on long-distance journeys by road and ferry. Her skills at producing distinct, unique and diverse garments have reached epic proportions, and, in her own words, she has become a *prolific hooker.* These days, she's rarely seen anywhere without a crochet hook and a ball of wool.

On reaching the Belgian coast, we proceeded along the E40, over the French border, past Dunkirk and reached Calais well ahead of schedule. Following the *Tunnel sous la Manche* road signs, we soon arrived at the Calais shuttle terminal.

The French authorities had deployed their military just before the check-in booths. Approximately twenty soldiers in full combat gear had taken up positions along the approach lanes towards check-in. These guys were taking their roles very seriously. Some were lying on the ground; others were standing upright, whilst the remainder had adopted the prone firing position. The French soldiers had been equipped with FN P90 submachine guns and 3-ply premium disposable face coverings.

At check-in, the attendant quickly noticed we were ahead of our scheduled departure time and kindly offered us an earlier slot. With minimal fuss, we were then directed towards the French border police. Once clear of passport control, our last hurdle was the UK Border Force.

The authorities at Calais and Dover operate what's known as juxtaposed controls. This reciprocal arrangement between France and the UK means you clear both countries' border controls before boarding the shuttle rather than upon arrival after disembarkation. So, the UK passport checks came next. At this point, we were absolutely convinced that we would be directed to a designated search and sniff area for a complete and thorough interrogation and examination while simultaneously having our morning's German shopping receipts scutinised. But nothing of the sort happened. Nothing whatsoever.

"Passports, please." It was the first British accent we'd heard in over six weeks. The officer in the booth looked at both passports, handed them back, and said, *"Straight on, turn right, down the ramp, and you will be directed onto the train."* *"But don't you need to check these?"* I asked, showing him the QR codes on our phones. *"Straight on, turn right, down the ramp, to the train, please,"* he repeated, almost rolling his eyes.

The shuttle departed Calais dead on time, and 35 minutes later, it arrived in Folkestone. We simply drove off and onto the M20 motorway. There were absolutely no checks on arrival. No inspections of our QR codes by controllers in Hazmat suits. No sightings of response teams or operational health and safety support units, not even a single helicopter. It was that straightforward, footloose and carefree.

As we weren't due back home for about four more weeks, a spur-of-the-moment decision was made, right then and there, to head up to Scotland and spend our time hiking in the Highlands. Our Big Trip of 2020 was definitely the most unprepared, most improvised and most spontaneous ever.

When we finally got back to the Isle of Man, a Government Emergency Powers COVID-19 Direction Notice for all Isle Man resident arrivals was in effect. This ruling required (pursuant to Regulation 7 (12) of the Entry Restrictions Regulations) that returning residents:

"Proceed directly, on arrival at the Isle of Man, to the specified premises declared previously on the Health Declaration form as the location you will remain at for the duration of the 14-day self-isolation period."

Before boarding the ferry to the Isle of Man, we stocked up on pasta, rice, tinned food, long-life milk, energy bars, biscuits, tea, coffee, flour, booze, etc, in preparation for the 14 days of confinement.

The day after we got home, while emptying all our provisions from the camper, Daisy, my neighbour's nine-year-old daughter, appeared from around the corner. Standing two metres from my driveway, she looked at me sternly and then spoke in an authoritative tone.

"For the next two weeks, you and Claire must not cross that line." She was pointing at the edge of our driveway, which borders the footpath. *"You must not leave your house for anything for fourteen days."* A nine-year-old girl had just read me the riot act.

I thanked Daisy profusely for the legal advice and assured her I would fully comply with all the regulations. I also realised that, for the next fortnight, all our movements outdoors would come under close surveillance. Would life ever be the same again?

****

Chapter Two

Fears and frustrations, genetic mutations, locked down nations and novel vaccinations

During the remaining months of 2020, the Isle of Man was dubbed Freedom Island. *Sky News*, amongst other media outlets, covered the island's remarkable disposition compared to the rest of the British Isles.

"Just imagine being this close again," the Sky broadcaster announced as he covered the story from a busy local dance school. Residents met, mixed and hugged again, and life was totally normal. By comparison, just 35 miles across the Irish Sea, the population in the Republic of Ireland was under Tier 5 government lockdown. With large-scale police checkpoints mounted across the entire country, all non-essential businesses and shops were shut, and all indoor and outdoor events were banned. The Irish population would be permitted to move, for exercise purposes only, within a 3.5-mile radius of their home. And, of course, it was a similar fate around the rest of the world.

We corresponded regularly with our friends in Germany and Greece, and it honestly felt like we were living on a different planet, just being in the Isle of Man. For so many, there was palpable fear and worry that it would get much worse before the proverbial light at the end of the tunnel shone through. I remember watching the news and broadcasts of the Isle of Man's annual Christmas lights celebrations from the island's capital, Douglas. The main street was packed with shoppers, and families were out enjoying the festive spirit. Brass bands played traditional Christmas carols, and street performers entertained the crowds. We also had loads of gigs throughout November and December, with Christmas parties, corporate events, pubs, hotels and clubs. It was rock 'n roll as usual. Then, suddenly, just after the first week of January 2021, the Manx bubble sprung a leak. We were back in a mini-lockdown, or a circuit breaker as they called it. It lasted less than three weeks before the pubs reopened again. I'm convinced, to this day, that the island's Chief Minister back then must have received a phone call from the British Prime Minister, Boris Johnson, with the following:

"Now steady on you lot. You're all having far too much fun and buffoonery on your rocky outcrop. It's enough to make a hog whimper. Enough of this confounded piffle, paffle, wiffle, waffle, and get locked down like the rest of us or face a naval blockade of your territorial waters."

Then, in March, we received an invitation from our local health services to get vaccinated. There had already been a lot of hype about so-called immunity passports to get the travelling world back on track. And whilst it had never been officially stated, it was widely assumed, by nearly everyone, that international travel would only be possible if your arm had been double jabbed, followed by a booster or three. The travel industry also called for more accurate nose swab molecular tests (PCR tests) to facilitate international trips.

We flat refused to get vaccinated and thus declined the invitation. It's a personal choice, and that, to quote Forrest Gump, *"is all I have to say about that."*

****

Having missed out on the joys of Greece in 2020, we were hell-bent, bound and determined to get there in 2021. And if that involved getting our noses swabbed at every border crossing, then so be it. Many concerns had even been raised over the effectiveness of travel restrictions so late in the day. Aside from almost bankrupting the travel industry, the restrictions didn't stop the spread of the virus. This was the conclusion of a study in *Science* magazine. So we remained optimistic that we'd somehow be able to manoeuvre and navigate our way, unvaccinated, across Europe come summer 2021 and reach the shores of Greece.

The biggest hurdle we envisaged in the early part of that year was the latest initiative coming out of 10 Downing Street. In between parties, that weren't actually parties but work events with karaoke machines, the UK government had decided to completely shut the borders. It was now illegal to leave the country.

Exemptions were granted to those working in the medical and transport sectors and, of course, government officials. But another curious exemption was for owners of overseas properties, who may need to carry out maintenance work or prune their petunias. This curious exemption, of course, would have had nothing to do with the fact that Boris Johnson's biological father, Stanley, has a mountain villa on the Pelion peninsula in Greece, and the garden probably needed tending. No, of course, it didn't.

The UK travel ban would remain effective until May 17th, but our feet were itching regardless of that. So, on April Fool's Day, and with great enthusiasm, we booked ferry tickets to leave the Isle of Man. We had gigs booked until June 12th, so our departure date was set for two days later. The loose plan (our A to Z plan) was to travel for at least four months, with Greece the ultimate destination. The unused ferry ticket from Italy to Greece, which we had booked in 2020, was still valid, so we contacted the company, Anek Lines, and scheduled July 1st for that part of the journey. The rest of our planning would be done daily, as it was nigh impossible to predict what was around the next corner during those uncertain times.

So, on June 14th, we were sailing back to the UK on the first leg of our Big Trip 2021. On board that morning ferry there weren't many other passengers, especially for what would usually be a busy summer period. Travelling was still a low priority for many folks. Once again, we stopped over in Liverpool to catch up with Claire's family. On the outskirts of the city, near the village of Melling, a farm provides basic stopover facilities for campers. It's a super safe and convenient location for us to stay whilst visiting Liverpool.

It's strange how sometimes you don't fully realise what you have been missing until you get it back. That's how we felt when we reunited with our four lovely nieces. That's Lily, Amelia, and Aria, aged eleven, nine and four, respectively. And the latest addition, the four month old Olivia. We made room in our camper for the three older girls, and they joined us clutching sleeping bags, colouring books, crayons, dolls, toys, bracelet and jewellery-making kits and a month's supply of snacks. The farm/camper stop owner allowed us to park in a nearby meadow, and he even hooked our van up with a long trailing electric cable. We spent two fun-packed days and nights with those crazy kids, and it was just the best start to our trip. It definitely brought normality back into our lives. The grass had been recently cut in the meadow where we were parked, making an excellent field for a game or two of rounders. We were treated to a gymnastics performance from Amelia followed by a fine display of cartwheels from the other two.

All around the world, just about everyone would be hoping and praying for some normality to return after the trauma and pain of lockdowns, restrictions and deprivations. The grief upon grief of not being able to attend a deceased loved one's funeral or visit an elderly relative in the hospital all contributed to higher levels of anguish and psychological distress. There's nothing normal about virtual-online-good-byes or standing in the pouring rain trying to talk, through a closed window, to an elderly loved one with dementia in a care home.

And, of course, children weren't immune either to the abnormal circumstances of this dark, Orwellian period. Overall, studies pointed to increased levels of distress, worry and anxiety, along with feelings of loneliness and worries about school and the future. Social restrictions, forcing people to stay at home and away from friends and family, doubled the odds of mental health symptoms. Not to mention the spike in domestic violence, child abuse, alcohol and drug abuse, and suicides. The original meaning of the word lockdown, according to Webster's Dictionary, is: *"The confinement of prisoners to their cells for all or most of the day as a temporary security measure."*

The authoritarian decision to lock down an entire nation was unprecedented in public health history. It was also made without any prior scientific studies. Was it really following the science to lockdown millions of healthy people? The jury is still out.

The morning before leaving Liverpool, we had appointments at a screening clinic in the city centre. This was for the obligatory PCR tests, a prerequisite for entering France. This was the first time we had been on the receiving end of a nasopharyngeal swab shoved into both nostrils, causing the eyes to water. The tests cost £60 each, and the results would be emailed to us within 24 hours. They also had to be taken within 72 hours before arriving in France, so the clock was ticking once we'd settled the bill. We jumped the bus back to see Claire's mum Kathy, and after a quick brew, we said our farewells and made our way by bus and foot to the farm/camper stop at Melling. From there, we headed south, on the M6 motorway, towards Birmingham, followed by the M40 towards Oxford. We'd pre-booked our shuttle through the Eurotunnel for the following morning, so around late afternoon, we stopped in a car park for the night in Banbury, north of Oxford.

The results of our PCR test arrived the following morning, and both showed negative results. Hooray! We were both virus-free, non-contagious, uncontaminated and fully pasteurized. Satisfied that we had ticked all the correct boxes for our entry into France, we set off bright and early the following morning.

Along with the negative PCR test results, still valid for another 48 hours, we had dutifully printed off and completed, prior to leaving home, a ream of other obligatory COVID forms for exiting the UK and entering France.

These included:

- COVID-19 Control Exit checklist.
- Sworn Statement of Absence of COVID-19 symptoms and contact with confirmed cases.
- Certificate for travel to Metropolitan France.
- A sworn statement certifying reasons for travel.
- A sworn Declaration to transit France within 24 hours.

We even printed off extra forms in case the completed and signed forms contained any errors and had to be filled out again. However, one eventuality not included in our to-do checklist was the consequence of the UK leaving the EU, commonly referred to as *Brexit.*

On the approach to the Eurotunnel terminal at Folkestone, there was a long queue of trucks. All were waiting to get processed for entry into the European Union. This was the second year since the UK officially left the EU. What was once seamless travel was now a serious headache for hauliers and their truck drivers.

Checks and paperwork would have to be carried out on every vehicle, resulting in lengthy queues. The last time we had seen anything like this was at the main EU border crossing between Serbia and Croatia, where miles upon miles of trucks have to wait, year-round, for processing to continue their journeys. Truck drivers gather together, in small groups, all along the road to the border, chain-smoking, scratching their bellies, and chatting amongst themselves to while away the hours of indisputable boredom. Fortunately for us, the trucks at Folkestone were queuing in their dedicated lane, allowing all other traffic to proceed unhindered.

After check-in and British passport control, we moved on to the juxtaposed French border police checks. They asked for our passports…..and nothing else. No PCR test results, mandatory sworn statements, or certified declarations of COVID-free cleanliness. Once again, we felt utterly hoodwinked by formalities and regulations that amounted to nothing.

But then came the bombshell we had never expected. *"Vous êtes vacciné?"* asked the policemen, pointing at Claire, inquiring about her vaccination status. I answered him in French, telling him that neither of us was vaccinated but had negative test results from our PCR tests. *"Non."* he replied. *"She is British, not an EU citizen, and must be vaccinated to enter France."* From the corner of my peripheral vision, I could see Claire burying her head despairingly in her hands. *"But we are married."* I replied. *"I am Irish, an EU citizen and she is my wife."* The policeman studied Claire's passport again, then glanced at mine. *"But the family name is not the same in the passports,"* he responded. Claire's passport still displayed her maiden name.

Above my head, stuffed behind the sun visor, was a copy of EU Directive 2004/38/EC, or the Freedom of Movement Directive applicable to all members of the European Union and their family members. Our marriage certificate was also stashed up there behind the sun visor. As politely as possible, to avoid making any waves, I handed over the marriage certificate to prove that we were legally wed. I also gently alluded to the EU Directive that extended the rights of freedom of movement to a family member of an EU citizen. All our documents were returned to us, and we were permitted to continue to board the shuttle to Calais.

To this day, I am still unsure if that brief encounter with the French border bureaucracy was correct. I'd never read anywhere that UK passport holders could be denied entry for not being fully vaccinated. It also made no sense because we had both tested negative and had the PCR test results to prove it. But as with so many diktats and orders from that period, not much made any sense. Just like the next 24 hours. We were officially allowed 24 hours to transit the country. But it didn't mean we couldn't stop somewhere and get out for shopping or a coffee. If we were to catch COVID-19 in the interim 24 hours, surely we could potentially infect someone else anyway?

After arriving in Calais, we drove towards Mons, Belgium, and from there, we continued towards Luxembourg. With the clock adjusted one hour ahead on the continent, it was already past midday, and we had no intention of attempting to cross the vastness of France towards Switzerland or Italy in the remaining daylight hours.

Luxembourg, I'd discovered in my pre-planning for the trip, had adopted a less draconian approach than neighbouring countries. For example, Belgium was still in transit-only mode, and Germany was completely out of bounds unless you had proof of a COVID-19 vaccination or recovery from infection. Luxembourg had no restrictions for land travel, and we crossed the border with no problems at all.

I'd pre-booked two nights at a campsite about 10 miles south of the city centre, and we arrived there late afternoon. We were actually feeling very relieved and relaxed to have made it thus far. The panic at the border over Claire's status had long subsided, and we were now definitely two chilled-out travellers in motion on a journey to somewhere bright and beautiful.

A barrier blocked our entry into the campsite, so I parked just in front, turned off the engine, and made my way to the office. With passports in my hand and a blue mask on my face, I entered the office. Just inside, I immediately detected the whiff of stale cigarette smoke. It was actually much stronger than just a whiff and seemed to permeate the entire office. In front of me was a large protective acrylic sneeze shield that sealed off the entire counter area up to the ceiling. A small hatch with a sliding acrylic door was the only accessible part of this defensive barrier.

After a few moments, I heard someone from beyond the sealed-off area arrive. A door opened, and a very thin woman with worried eyes appeared. I immediately noticed that she had fitted not one but two protective blue masks to her face and was wearing blue latex gloves. Despite the double face mask covering, I could detect an unhealthy ashen grey pallor. Her hair was pulled back in a bun, and her movements were slow and fatigued. She spoke to me in French in an almost bewildered tone.

"How can I help you?" she asked. I gave my name and explained that I had made a reservation for two nights at the campsite. *"Where are you from?"* she asked, hearing my foreign accent. *"Ireland,"* I replied, as it would have been too awkward to explain the location of the Isle of Man. Her eyes widened as she asked, *"But how did you get here from Ireland?"*

The question almost merited a witty reply, something like: *"We converted ourselves into energy patterns using a teleporter, then got beamed over, re-materialising here at the target destination."*

But this was not the time or place for any silliness. This woman appeared nervous and uneasy in the presence of her unexpected visitor. She asked for our passports whilst simultaneously sliding open the small plastic access door on the sneeze screen. I passed them through, and her gloved hand flicked them across the counter to a micro-fibre cleaning cloth. She then furiously wiped them down, both sides, before opening and turning to the information pages within. She slowly and methodically entered the information from our passports into a computer whilst I waited silently on the other side of the sneeze screen.

At this precise moment, I felt an annoying tickle starting at the back of my throat. It was nothing serious, just the urge to clear my throat and nothing more. Maybe the pungent smell of stale cigarette smoke in the office had triggered the tickle? Or a loose fibre from my face mask had dislodged itself and was now nestled at the back of my throat? I had no idea, but the more I suppressed the itch the stronger the urge to cough increased. I couldn't bear it any longer, so I covered my mouth with my hand and attempted to perform a very gentle *a-hem*. It was a one-syllable-type *a-hem*, a kind of low-key rumble. But it didn't do the trick. And even though it had been a feeble attempt at cough suppression, the double-masked woman stopped and stared with a vexed glare visible from the unmasked portion of her face. With the itchy sensation persisting, I had to have another go, only this time it was a much louder woof.

"Monsieur." she snapped, clearly very irritated,

before turning to finish off the registration process, shaking her head indignantly. I then had to sign the registration form and slide it back through the hatch, which also got the micro-fibre treatment. Payment for the two nights was required upfront, and the only accepted method was by debit card. With these formalities out of the way, I asked if there was a specific pitch or plot where we had to park our camper. She replied, *"Wherever you want, you are the only visitors here."*

But before exiting the office, I was given a full and detailed explanation of the sanitation block, its location and opening times. The showers and wash areas were only accesible during certain hours of the day and were limited to three persons per visit. Social distancing had to be observed at all times while inside the facilities. As we were the only guests on the entire site, this wouldn't present any immediate difficulties.

I returned to the camper just as the entrance barrier in front automatically lifted, allowing us to drive into the campsite. Once we passed the barrier, we pulled over to assess our pitch options. With so many choices, it was pretty challenging. Next to the sanitary block would be handy for the showers and toilets, I thought. But Claire preferred going further along and parking next to a neat hedge.

In the end, we comprised and picked a pitch offering both a neat hedge and close proximity to the shower block. It didn't take us long to get the camper manoeuvred into position and hooked up to the electricity. We rolled the awning out, arranged the table and chairs and enjoyed a much-needed coffee.

The peace and quiet, in the warmth of the afternoon sun, was exhilarating. We'd made it all the way to Luxembourg in one day, fully intact and with no repercussions apart from my throat tickle. It was a milestone. We were confident that the rest of the journey to Greece would be plain sailing. All we had to do was decide which route would be best.

The obvious choice would be straight south via Nancy to Switzerland and on to Milan. But Switzerland could possibly be very twitchy at the border with controls, bureaucracy and, most certainly, a whole set of new travel regulations. The other option was to travel south-west across France, around Switzerland and into Italy that way.

As I sipped my coffee, contemplating our route options, I glanced back towards the office. The woman from reception had stepped outside and was now sitting in the shade, smoking vigorously. Between puffs, I could see that she was carefully realigning the two face masks to defend against any noxious microbes drifting in the vicinity. Seconds after finishing one cigarette she sparked up another. She was definitely a 60-a-day lass. This explained the smell of stale cigarette smoke in the office. She was the source of the acrid, woody odour. The pervading, musty stench had been permeating from her skin pores into the enclosed office environment.

The next morning, we set off on our bikes along the banks of the River Alzette towards Luxembourg City. It was another beautiful sunny day, perfect for our visit to the medieval old town. As we reached the outskirts, the old quarters and fortifications ahead made such an impressive sight. On that sunny morning, it was even more impressive for us as the narrow streets and squares were practically deserted. We had to dismount and push the bikes up a very narrow cobblestone walkway to reach the ramparts. From there, it was a short walk to the old town.

Normally, the streets and tourist attractions would be buzzing with visitors from all over the world. But there were very few other visitors to be seen that morning. The atmosphere, however, was very relaxed and laid back, especially inside the numerous small shops selling tourist trinkets, T-shirts and postcards. We even saw smiles again, as there was no mask mandate to enter the stores.

After all the concerns and unease to get this far, it was very pleasant and welcoming to see. So much so that we decided, then and there, to stay another two nights. Maybe the delight and enjoyment of feeling that sense of normality once again swung it for us. As we cycled back along the River Alzette to the campsite, I made a mental note: *"I love Luxembourg."*

On arrival back at the campsite, the first thing I did was pay a visit to the office and settle the bill for another two nights. The smoky, thin lady was much more affable and quite chatty with me this time around, even asking how our day had been.

She went on to tell me that a Dutch couple had arrived earlier with a caravan and were parked just beyond our pitch. I glanced out the office window, and sure enough, there was a caravan next to a black Audi hatchback with a familiar yellow Netherlands registration.

In this vast and empty campsite, the best pitch they could find for their caravan and car was right next to us. I wasn't complaining to myself or having any anti-social thoughts; I was merely thinking how odd it was to park right on the other side of our hedge when there was an abundance of other vacant pitches, all with neat hedges.

Before I left the office, the smoky, thin lady proudly told me about the country's free public transport system. In Luxembourg, all the trains, buses and trams are completely free of charge. This generous government freebie also extends to the city's funicular railway connecting the Pfaffenthal district to the Kirchberg Plateau. As an extra bonus, there is no charge for luggage or pets either.

Back at the camper, I could hear the chop-chop of Claire dicing onions and mushrooms in preparation for our staple meal of the evening. Spaghetti with chopped vegetables in a pasta sauce. I told her all about the free public transport, finishing my words with, *"Isn't it just brilliant here?"* I heard the fizz-pop of a can of beer opening, and then Claire stepped outside with a glass and a can for me, saying, *"From now on, you have to pay one euro every time you say that."* *"Say what?"* I asked. *"Isn't it just brilliant here?"* she replied, *"You've said it about a hundred times today."* Oh well, memo to self, *"I love Luxembourg."*

The following day, we set off again on the bikes to explore the surrounding countryside. And on the fourth day, we just relaxed outside the camper in the warm summer air. It was a chance to sort through all the photos we'd taken from Luxembourg and for me to post a big write-up to our Rocking Life on the Road Facebook travel page.

Claire had started the travel page three years earlier, and we had already amassed 1,200 followers by the summer of 2021. There were also quite a few private messages for me to answer. They were mainly from eager, like-minded travellers enquiring about restrictions and regulations we had encountered while leaving the UK.

From our serene surroundings in this peaceful corner of Luxembourg, I'd almost forgotten all about PCR tests, personal locator forms, checklists, declarations, and sworn testimonies. Nevertheless I answered all the messages as honestly as possible from our experiences and where we had been so far. Obviously, I couldn't account for what was happening in other parts of Europe.

This brought me back to earth and the planning of our next move. We would be leaving the campsite, with lovely neat hedges, the following morning, and we still hadn't formulated a proper plan. Getting to Ancona would involve a two or three days drive, depending on the chosen route. There were also the entry requirements for Greece for us to consider.

Introduced in May 2021, all travellers to Greece had to complete a PLF before entry. This involved providing detailed information on departure points, the duration of previous stays in other countries, and a contact address in Greece. The application had to be submitted online no later than 24 hours before arrival, and once processed, a QR code would be sent via email. Also, for the non-vaccinated, it was mandatory to present a negative molecular test for COVID-19, carried out in the 72 hours before arrival in the country. This last requirement was the one that concerned us the most.

In France, there were screening centres located in most towns and cities where all members of the public could go and get tested free of charge. Called *Dépistage du COVID-19*, the screening centres were open between the usual working hours Monday to Friday, and a few also offered the service on Saturday mornings. However, for Italy, I simply couldn't find any information on screening centres or laboratories where we could get a PCR test done. Being able to speak French proved invaluable at this time, as I was able to call ahead for details, book appointments if required, ask for directions, and find our way around. That luxury would be lost to us in Italy, as neither of us spoke a word of the language, and, in our experience, not many Italians spoke anything but Italian.

On Friday, June 25th, we left the campsite and headed towards France. In my diary from that day, I wrote: *"Both of us were feeling nervous. It's just the uncertainty of all this stuff and the awful control it inflicts on our lives. The four days in Luxembourg had been so relaxing and normal that we had momentarily forgotten what was horribly called the New Normal."*

Just over the border, the French police had set up a temporary road checkpoint, but they were merely observing the traffic as we drove past. Thirty minutes later, we arrived in the small city of Thionville. Earlier that morning, I had called ahead to a *Dépistage du COVID-19* to arrange our PCR tests.

No appointment was necessary, and the whole process was quick, friendly, and efficient. I was told that the results would be sent via email within the next 24 hours. Our ferry to Greece was scheduled for the following Monday at 3:30 p.m., but that was more than 72 hours away. The Greek entry regulations stated quite clearly that a negative PCR test had to be carried out within 72 hours prior to arrival. Plus, there was the ferry time to Greece, which was an extra 19 hours.

On the way back to the camper, I told Claire, *"We've miscalculated the times. We'll have to do another test somewhere and ensure we have enough time to reach Greece within 72 hours."*

Before leaving Thionville, we had to stock up on food supplies. So we found a huge supermarket on the outskirts, where Claire headed off with a trolley and a long shopping list. I stayed with the camper and checked the map.

The French city of Mulhouse was 180 miles south of Thionville and only 20 miles from there to the Swiss border. Most importantly, a *Dépistage du COVID-19* laboratory in Mulhouse was open on Saturday mornings.

But I still had that nagging negative feeling about possible Swiss bureaucracy at the border. On the official Swiss Government website, British citizens had to be isolated for 10 days on arrival. But I couldn't find any information about transiting in a camper van. And because Switzerland is not in the EU, would they permit Claire, with her British passport, to transit through the country with her Irish/EU husband? It was all a bit of a grey area, really.

So, whilst Claire was still away shopping, I glanced over the map towards Nancy, Dijon, Lyon, Chambéry and a route into Italy circumnavigating Switzerland altogether. We could get re-tested at a lab in Chambéry late on Saturday morning, and that would hopefully give us enough time, within the 72-hour deadline, to get to Ancona and on to Greece.

While mulling these new options, my peripheral vision caught a middle-aged couple standing close by, pointing at the camper's registration number. The man looked up, smiled, and then turned to walk towards me. So I stepped outside, and we quickly engaged in light-hearted banter about the whereabouts of the Isle of Man and the unusual registration number that he'd never seen the like of before.

The Isle of Man has its own vehicle registration system and our number, with the *Three Legs of Mann flag,* always arouses curiosity and intrigue wherever we travel.

The couple were very friendly and asked several questions about our visit to France, where we had been, where we were going, etc. I told the couple that our destination was Greece, but I had reservations about transiting through Switzerland.

The guy shrugged his shoulders and said, *"Monsieur. Why don't you drive to Italy via Nancy, Dijon, Lyon, and Chambéry?"* He continued, *"That way, you avoid going through Switzerland, and the scenery after Chambéry is magnificent. It is the Auvergne-Rhône-Alpes and it runs into the Piedmont region of Italy. C'est tout à fait magnifique."*

At that precise moment, I saw Claire pushing an overflowing shopping trolley from the supermarket. I thanked the friendly Frenchman for his top tip of the day, wished him and his wife a bonne journée, and went to help Claire with the shopping.

"Guess what. There's a change of plan. We're not going through Switzerland now," I told her excitedly. She replied, *"Oh, I bought some extra packets of spaghetti and pasta sauce and that stinky cheese you like, plus extra wine,"* not even acknowledging this major detour. She had become oblivious to last-minute changes, U-turns, one-eighties, turnabouts, flip-flops, and significant deviations.

We drove for about eight hours that day, stopping for the night on a fabulous free camper park at Bourg-en-Bresse, the capital of the ancient province of Bresse in the Auvergne-Rhône-Alpes region of Eastern France. Along the way, we stopped to book our next COVID test at a screening centre in Chambéry for the following day at 1:00 p.m. On the phone, the receptionist told me that it was the last appointment of the day and to be aware that all the screening clinics would be shut until the following Monday. This would be our last chance to get tested before our mad dash across Italy. Also, the test would fall within the confines of the 72-hour deadline imposed by the Greek authorities. Based on the timing of our test results, I even calculated that we would arrive in Greece with about five hours to spare.

It's about 100 miles from Bourg-en-Bresse to Chambéry, so we were up and away at the crack of dawn, arriving around 11:00 am, in plenty of time for what would be our last free nasopharyngeal COVID swab in France.

The receptionist we encountered at the screening centre was a feminine humanoid robot type. She functioned entirely by the book, almost mechanically. Lacking any social interaction or skills, she directed us to separate booths to wait for the swabber. After completing the tests, we nodded goodbye to the fembot at reception, who completely blanked us, returned to the camper and reached our destination around 5:30 p.m.

Alessandria is about 50 miles east of Turin and, for the night, Claire had located a *Parcheggio gratuito per Camper,* or free camper park, in the city with all the facilities so that was good enough for us.

The drive, earlier that day, up from the alpine town of Chambéry through the Auvergne-Rhône-Alpes région was simply magnificent. The Alps still had snow on top whilst the outside temperature was hovering around 30 degrees Celsius. The friendly Frenchman, back in Thionville, was absolutely correct when he said to me: *"C'est tout à fait magnifique."*

We had reached the Fréjus road tunnel, which connects France and Italy, by mid-afternoon. The tunnel runs under Col du Fréjus in the Cottian Alps and is approximately eight miles long. It is one of the major trans-Alpine transport routes, and for the convenience of using this 8-mile-long tunnel, the toll charge was an eye-watering 62 euros one way. That's 7.75 euros per mile.

Speechless and a tad traumatised, we handed over the toll payment and entered the subterranean road immediately ahead of us. Nine minutes and thirty-six seconds later, we exited. The light at the end of the tunnel had literally been the glorious afternoon sunshine over the Piedmont region of Italy.

It was a beautiful evening at our *Parcheggio gratuito per Camper* in Alessandria. We sat outside in the lovely warm air all evening, sipping white wine with a full orchestra of chirping crickets in the background. We felt thoroughly contented and happy with our progress since leaving Luxembourg. It had all gone to a last-minute plan, and from here, there were only another 500 miles to Ancona and our ferry to Greece.

We left Alessandria about 9:30 the following morning for a non-stop motorway journey toward Piacenza, then on to Parma and Bologna, arriving late afternoon in Forli, a city in the Emilia-Romagna region of Italy. Once again,

Claire found a free camper park for our last night in Italy. From Forli, we still had another 100 miles remaining to reach Ancona, which was a mere doddle of a drive considering the 1500 miles we'd already covered to get this far.

Only one last hurdle remained: the Greek PLF that had to be completed 24 hours before travelling. It was already past four o'clock in the afternoon so that was *about 24 hours* before travelling. While Claire filled out the online PLF form, I checked emails and immediately saw the test results from Chambéry had landed in my inbox. Both results were negative, and a quick calculation showed that we still had 45 hours before the expiry deadline. In 24 hours' time, we'd be on the ferry to Greece; factor in the 19 hours of sailing time, and we'd arrive in Igoumenitsa with two hours to spare. I punched the air with great satisfaction and gave Claire the updated and amended spare hours prediction just as she clicked the submit button on the completed Greek PLF form.

"Why don't you go and check out the camper park, love? See what facilities there are. I'll get the dinner started." This was code for make yourself useful and take the rubbish to the bin.

I took a stroll around the deserted camper park and located the recycling bins, the freshwater tap, the greywater drainage point, and the toilet disposal area. It never ceases to amaze me how motorhomes and camper vans are so well catered for in France, Germany, Italy, and many other European countries. Many of these facilities are completely free of charge, and those that do levy a fee never ask for more than 10 or 15 euros on average.

As I returned to the camper from my reconnaissance mission to the recycling zone, I could hear the familiar chop-chop sounds of onions and mushrooms being diced up for the default spaghetti with chopped vegetables in a pasta sauce. And, as I got within close range, I heard the fizz-pop of a can of cold beer being opened for me from within. What a lucky guy I am.

The table and chairs were already outside; all that remained was for me to roll out the awning and set the table for dinner. Our last night in Italy was so beautifully quiet and peaceful. After a few glasses of wine and a couple of games of backgammon, we hit the hay, exhausted from this adventure so far, and slept like logs until the early morning.

We left Forli just after 08:00 the following morning and headed straight to Ancona, arriving around 10:30. We needed LPG gas, so I spotted a filling station on the way to the port and pulled over at the gas pump. We have a self-refillable gas cylinder system built into our camper with an assortment of different EU gas nozzle adapters. This LPG system is factory-fitted, fully tested, serviced and approved.

Nevertheless, just as I was screwing on the appropriate adapter, a guy came running over towards us, waving his arms and snarling in Italian, *"Non è consentito riempire bombole di gas."* His angry face alone convinced us that self-filling gas bottles in Italy was a big no-no. This is crazy because the system is so safe and foolproof. Come to think of it, it's probably safer than filling a car with petrol. After that minor incident, we drove straight to the sea terminal, where we had to check-in and collect our ferry tickets.

Outside the offices, a full-on entry protocol was in place. With my face mask on, hands sanitised, and socially distanced, I joined the queue and waited my turn to enter. The uniformed guard at the entrance must have been a child maths prodigy as he could calculate the exact number of people already inside the building at any given time. He accomplished this feat of ingenuity even though the entrance was situated around the corner and about 50 metres from the exit gates. Just by a mere glance inside the terminal building, he was able to assess the number of passengers milling around and when it was *safe* to enter. There was clearly no system in place, and this was all just pure theatre.

When I was allowed to proceed, I entered a huge and busy reception area. There were signs everywhere for different destinations: Durres (Albania), Split, Stari Grad/Hvar, Zadar (Croatia), Trieste and Venice (Italy). Then I spotted Corfu/Igoumenitsa/ Patras (Greece) and went straight to the ticket window.

Our vehicle documents, passports, PLF submissions, negative COVID tests, etc., had to be presented to the young lady at check-in. We had booked camping on board, which meant we'd be parked on an open deck with an electric hook-up and allowed to stay in the camper for the whole voyage. This was a much better option than booking a cabin and dining on board. She returned all documents to me, then printed out the tickets, passing them through the slot in the clear plastic sneeze screen. Then she casually said, in a strong, disconnected, Italian accent, *"Inbound ferry delayed - New departure time 17:00 - Have a nice trip - Ciao."*

I felt my carotid arteries double pulsate at this news. I said nothing; I just grabbed the tickets and headed for the unmanned exit doors, dodging fellow travellers shuffling into the building, via the exit doors, un-checked.

As I made my way back to the camper, I quickly calculated that our PCR tests would no longer have two hours to spare on arrival. They would have only 30 minutes remaining, and that was on the presumption that there'd be no further delays.

After telling Claire the news, we both decided it wasn't worth worrying about any of this anymore. We had done absolutely everything in our power to meet the requirements. It was hardly our fault that Anek Ferry Lines couldn't provide a punctual service. And if we arrived in Greece late, effectively invalidating our test results, the Greeks could test us again, then and there.

A guy in a high-visibility vest directed us towards a vast parking area beyond Port Security. We were the first vehicle in lane and the only other vehicle waiting in line for quite some time. Arriving five hours before the scheduled departure time probably explained this. So we put the kettle on, the deck chairs came out, and we positioned ourselves on the shady side of the camper with our coffees.

Over the next few hours, the huge parking area filled up with more and more cars and vans. A big green self-built camper had parked just behind us, and a German guy with a large girth came over to ask about our registration number plate. I took an instant dislike to him after he explained he was travelling to Greece only because he enjoyed the weather. He had a deep aversion for the Greek people and didn't seem a bit bothered by his rank discrimination and bigotry.

He even boasted about all the German beer he had brought, along with an abundant supply of canned bratwurst and dried food from his local Lidl store. It was almost like he didn't even want to spend a single cent in Greece, as doing so would only help the country's economy. Just as I was about to make a quick getaway and escape his narcissistic personality disorder, he changed the subject to his journey from southern Germany. He told me that he'd driven via Switzerland to Italy.

Unfortunately, I was too curious, so I had to ask if there had been any fuss at the Swiss border with COVID-19 regulations. *"Nein."* he answered. *"I am fully vaccinated, so no problems for me, nicht wahr?"* Then came the almost predictable question of the day: *"So, what about you? Are you also fully vaccinated?"* When I told him I had declined the invitation to get jabbed, his facial expression immediately displayed fierce disapproval, almost hostility. Then, with small rearward steps, he backed away towards his camper, muttering indignantly in German.

Apart from the dark days when pedestrians would hurl themselves into oncoming traffic to avoid other pedestrians walking in the opposite direction, it was the first time I'd encountered palpable fear of the unvaccinated.

The good news was that our ferry, the *Hellenic Spirit*, wasn't further delayed, and around 5:00 p.m., we were, indeed, on our way. Parked right next to the ship's side, the views leaving Italy were just amazing.

As the sun set across the Mediterranean and the Italian coast disappeared from sight, we headed inside for a very restful night. Before drifting off to sleep, I felt a deep sense of contentment and achievement. We had jumped through all the hoops, pulled out all the stops and fulfilled our dream of travelling back to beautiful Greece. And in just one more sleep, we'd be there.

****

Chapter Three

First three weeks in Greece

Around 08:00 in the morning, the *Hellenic Spirit* docked on the Greek island of Corfu. After the disembarkation and embarkation of several vehicles and a small group of passengers, we were back en route to the port of Igoumenitsa, arriving around noon. By the time we rolled off the ferry, got stopped, and checked by the Greek police, we had only 15 minutes remaining on our 72-hour deadline. The cop flicked through our passports, glancing several times at the PCR test results before instructing us to *"Go and see the doctor in the clinic."*

We drove about 100 metres beyond the police checkpoint but couldn't see anything that resembled a medical centre or clinic, so I pulled over and set off on foot. A few moments later, a door at the side of a building flew open, and two young nurses in blue medical scrubs stepped outside.

"Yassas! Can we help you?" I told them that the port police had sent us over to see them. They both smiled back, and one nurse said, *"No problem. Happy holidays!"* And that was it. The nurses hadn't asked for anything or checked our documents or health status, and just like that, we were out of the port and on our way. Welcome to Greece!

Just beyond the port perimeter, I spotted a petrol station displaying the availability of LPG, so we stopped there to fill our gas bottles. The attendant who came out smiled and greeted us with a *"Yassas!"* followed by a familiar question, *"Where are you from?"* pointing at the registration number. There were no hysterics or angry words about filling our gas bottles. As soon as I'd fitted the correct adapter to the filler point, he merely asked, *"Full?"* followed by a palm down, left to right-hand movement. This is a customary Greek hand signal meaning: fill to capacity. I answered him with a *"Naí gemáto parakaló"* or *"Yes, full, please."* He broke out in a big grin and said, *"You speak Greek?"* I explained that I'd been learning his language for several years now and had experienced several bouts of madness, neurasthenia and psychotic episodes as a consequence. Greek grammar will do that to you.

He wanted to know all about our trip and where we would be visiting in Greece. When I told him the Prespes Lakes, he immediately nodded his approval and exclaimed, *"Po, po, po, polý oraío"* or *"Wow, wow, wow, very nice."* Another customary Greek hand gesture followed this. It's the fingers and thumb of the right hand pressed together gesture, pointing upwards, followed by a slight backwards and forwards swaying motion. The gesture represents the full endorsement, the rubber stamping, of an idea, proposal, or achievement.

With the gas bottles topped up and our purchase paid for, I asked the cheerful attendant if I could fill the camper's fresh water tank. *"Of course! No problem!"* came the reply as he pointed me toward a forecourt corner where I could see a long yellow hose pipe. With our water tank full and a quick shop for food provisions, we were on our way to one of the most spectacular corners of Greece, if not all of Europe.

****

The Prespa Lakes and National Park.

Located in the far Northwestern corner of the country, in the region of West Macedonia, Prespa National Park covers an area of 126 square miles and consists of two lakes, Megali and Mikri Prespa or Big and Small Prespa. It's a protected area and is considered an ecosystem of global significance. The lakes are home to the most significant breeding colony of Dalmatian Pelicans in the world. But that's only one part of the story.

There is also an unusually high number of plant and fauna species, including insects, mammals, fish, and birds, many of them endemic to the area. From the surrounding high mountains and alpine meadows down to the wetland habitats and lakes the sheer number of species is quite unique. In recent years, the following has been observed and recorded at Prespa National Park:

2,000 species of flora
271 bird species
60 mammal species
23 fish species (nine of which are endemic to the area)
22 reptile species & 11 amphibians.

There is even a small blue butterfly that flutters around the forests and fauna here, and it has an extraordinary symbiotic relationship with ants. The butterfly's larvae drop to the ground from branches, where they wait to be picked up by passing ants, who then take them back to their nests and care for them. The blue butterfly achieves this amazing free fostering trick by fooling the ants into rearing its young by masking them with the ants' own smell. The mountains surrounding the lakes are also among the last European homes for brown bears and grey wolves.

Our drive there, from Igoumenitsa, took over five hours through the northern range of the Pindus Mountains. From Kastoria, it is approximately 45 miles further along a winding mountainous road to Florina.

Halfway along this route, at the settlement of Trigono, there is another uphill road full of twists and turns, which takes you all the way to the lakes. This road is one way in and one way out. There is no other route to circumnavigate or bring you back out. Albania and the Former Yugoslav Republic of Macedonia also lie ahead, but there are no border crossings anywhere or provisions to continue further.

At the top of the highest point of this road, the vista ahead is simply breathtaking. In the distance, you can see the twin lakes and wetlands, surrounded by high mountains and forests. Every time I visit here, I experience a surge of emotions.

However, in an ironic twist, my joy, happiness and exuberance are mixed with a marked melancholy. Like so many other fragile areas of our planet, the Prespa Lakes region is threatened by many ecological and environmental threats. The water level in the larger lake has fallen by more than nine metres in the last 70 years. This is largely due to milder winters with less snowfall on the mountains, which would normally replenish the lake after hot, short summers. However, increased irrigation and misuse of water have also contributed to the problems. Uncontrolled forest use, cutting firewood for heating, hunting and illegal fishing, and the non-management of urban waste and sewage are also factors leading to the deterioration of Prespa's ecosystems.

And then there is the history of destructive human conflicts, invasions, and wars that have scarred the psyche and soul of the land. On previous visits, I have often listened to stories from some local people about the suffering due to wars, hardships, evacuations, and expulsions. Sorrowful experiences that are no longer visibly conspicuous but still endure in the memories of those who lived through them.

From the top of this highest point, the road winds down until it reaches a long straight section, passing the villages of Lefkonas and Plati before stopping at a T-junction. Quite a few old, run-down stone buildings and abandoned dwelling places are scattered around the landscape. Overgrown wooden gazebos that once served as shelters from the sun deteriorate by discarded viewpoints. Old derelict tavernas, long closed down due to lack of trade, lie next to neglected public areas in a stark reminder of the region's economic decline. It's abundantly clear that Prespas has already enjoyed a more prosperous period.

At the T-junction, a right turn leads to the villages of Laimos and Agios Germanos. To the left, the road passes across a narrow isthmus separating the two lakes. This section of the road is locally referred to as the Koula. There are about another 12 miles before the road comes to a full stop at a village called Vrondero. The Koula isthmus and surrounding land were once completely submerged as the twin lakes were once one large body of water. I have been shown old black-and-white photos that attest to this fact. One elderly gentleman in Laimos once told me how, as a young child, the lake water would reach halfway up to his knees as he waded along the Koula isthmus.

About two miles further on, there is another turn-off to the right. This turn leads up a very steep, windy road on a mountain known as Devas. I've counted sixteen sharp bends on the way up and a similar number on the way down. At the highest point, there is a chapel called Agios Georgios, and at the bottom, next to the lake, is the beautiful old traditional fishing village of Psarades.

We arrived late afternoon and made a left turn at the T-Junction. We would typically drive straight to Psarades, but this time, we decided to rest for the night behind an old, closed-down taverna at the end of the Koula.

This taverna, once upon a time, enjoyed a roaring local and tourist trade when the lake's water level reached right up to the rear of the building. Visitors could go swimming and enjoy water sports, followed by drinks and meals in the large outdoor seating area. These days, the shoreline has receded by at least 150 metres, and a large reed bed has sprung up, practically making the lake inaccessible to any budding bathers. And what was once a lakebed is now a large sloping sandy beach covered in thorny shrubs and grasses.

It's solid ground, for the most part, and we've parked several times there in the past. However, this time, I made one manoeuvre too many, and the camper's front wheels dug themselves deep into the soft ground. There is very little other traffic in such a remote area, and we were miles from the nearest roadside assistance service. But help was close at hand. Like those migratory Dalmatian Pelicans, we, too, have become migratory visitors here, and our annual presence hasn't gone unnoticed. In other words, we've made some solid friendships over the years, and this was about to be put to the test. I grabbed my phone from the front of the camper and called the lovely Eleni in Psarades.

Eleni, her brother Christos, and their parents own a small taverna called *Ta Paragádia* or *The Longlines* and serve the most delicious, authentic Greek food imaginable.

"Where are you?" she asked, hearing my voice on the other end of the line. *"Stuck,"* I replied. I then continued, explaining exactly what had happened and where we were. *"Don't worry, Derek. I'll send Christos."*

About 15 minutes later, a small car appeared down the dusty trail towards where we were marooned. It was Eleni's father, and after a hearty welcome and hugs all around, he diligently assessed our predicament. Then he took his phone out and called his son to explain the situation. Christos arrived shortly after in his 4x4 pick-up truck, wearing a big grin and an Isle of Man T-shirt—a gift we had sent him the previous year. *"You have a problem?"* he laughed loudly. Followed by, *"Look at my nice T-shirt. It's a perfect fit!"*

Christos is taller than a large tree and built like a concrete blockhouse. He has a vice-like handshake and a bear hug that could crush bones. A chest bump from this guy could easily send the recipient into a low Earth orbit. As I recovered from his formidable body lock and sensed an improved circulation to my right hand, Christos set about attaching a towrope between the camper and his truck. Back behind the steering wheel, I felt the gentle tug of the towrope as Christos reversed his truck. A second later, the camper was free from its sand pit.

Cheers and high fives followed as we celebrated the recovery and our return to more solid ground. Christos and his Dad then zoomed off up the mountainside towards Psarades while we secured the inside of the camper and quickly followed them up the same mountain.

Eleni and her Mum were all smiles and laughter as we arrived at their taverna. *"Entáxei Derek? Ola kalá?"* I smiled and said we were doing very well and very happy to be back again. We sat at our favourite table and ordered food, along with a couple of beers. A Greek salad with feta cheese arrived, followed by grilled chicken, fried potatoes, tzatziki, a portion of keftedákia or meatballs, and a plate of Tsironia, small grilled fish.

The keftedákia, made by Eleni's Mum, has always been a firm favourite of ours. Along with the other dishes, we had ourselves a feast.

We were the only customers at the taverna, and it was a stark reminder of how these small, out-of-the-way places struggle to survive. Even during the years before COVID, we've never seen throngs of tourists visiting any of the Prespa tavernas and cafés.

We chatted with Christos and Eleni for a few hours before returning to the camper. When I went to pay, they stopped me, and, with the flat of his hand placed over his heart, Christos said, *"No. This time, it is from us. Welcome back to Psarades!"* Greek hospitality, especially from those in less prosperous circumstances, never fails to knock us sideways. The kindest people I've ever met are from this wonderful country's remote, rural areas.

The village is on one side of a narrow bay, and we always park on the opposite side. Once back at our improvised pitch, we sat outside under the stars, with a glass of wine each, staring at the twinkling lights across the bay. The sounds of cicadas and other nighttime bugs, along with the croaking symphony of frogs communicating from the lakeside reed beds, filled the warm air. It all looked so peaceful and tranquil, and that about also summed up our mood.

We had made it. Over 1,800 miles of road travel since leaving the Isle of Man two weeks earlier. All our concerns and anxieties, the PCR tests and personal locator forms, the QR codes, permits and sworn testimonies, vanished into the warm night air above Psarades. We were blissfully content and happy and had no intention of moving another mile for at least a couple of weeks.

The following morning, bright and early, we unhooked our e-bikes and set off up the steep road out of Psarades. Down on the other side, we turned left onto the Koula, cycling past the old taverna where we had got stuck the night before, past the T-Junction and then to the village of Laimos.

On our way there, we spotted a shepherd with a large flock of sheep in a nearby field. As we cycled past, three large, angry dogs came lunging from the roadside at our bikes. Barking and snarling, they followed us for a short distance before giving up and returning to the flock.

It startled us, especially as the shepherd didn't seem bothered about the incident. At a safe distance, I got off my bike and shouted over to him while gesturing towards the dogs. He came over, but I couldn't understand a word from his toothless, grinning mouth. I realised he was Albanian and probably hired by a local farmer to tend the sheep. So we got back on our bikes and continued to Laimos.

On previous visits, we'd made friends with a few of the elderly Greeks who sit each morning at a café in the village square. We parked our bikes and went for a coffee and, sure enough, old familiar faces smiled and greeted us back. These opportunities were just what I needed to help my Greek along. Even though the local accents are strong, and sometimes a regional dialect called *topikó* is spoken, I can still understand and speak to them. Most of the time, we just exchanged small talk and humorous banter, but I hoped to dig a bit deeper and learn more about them and the history of the surrounding villages.

Every other day, we would return to Laimos and meet up with the Wise Men of the Village, as I jokingly referred to them.

One elderly man often present when we arrived for our coffees became increasingly interested in us. He spoke very softly, clearly, and, most importantly, very slowly. I could understand him so well, and if there were any words that I was unsure of, he'd take the time to rephrase so I could understand.

From then on, I looked forward very much to meeting him and listening to all his past stories. Then, one day, we were invited to his home further out the road towards the village of Agios Germanos. The invite was for the following morning at 10:00. *"At the small house, on the right, with the Greek flag flying."*

When we arrived, he'd prepared a small round table in his garden with four chairs under a large parasol. A timid and diminutive lady appeared from the house, extending her hand and welcoming us in Greek. It was his wife Magdalína, and her husband went by the name of Vangelis.

Magdalína returned inside to prepare coffees whilst Vangelis gave us the full tour of his garden. Tomatoes, cucumbers, courgettes, aubergines, fruits, lots of herbs and flowers all grew profusely in neat rows whilst chickens roamed freely, picking and scratching around in the soil for bugs and pests. They clearly served as mini-gardeners, mulching and *dropping* nutrient-rich fertiliser while providing free eggs.

As he walked down each row, Vangelis snipped and collected vegetables, placing them in a large bag. At the end of the garden tour, he presented us with a bag containing enough fresh produce for a week. Magdalína came out carrying an old metal tray with four strong Greek coffees and a plate of homemade biscuits. She also handed us a small bag with four large fresh eggs inside.

And once again, I felt overwhelmed by these small, random acts of kindness. The coffee and biscuits were lovely, as was the company. It was as if we were a million miles away from all the hustle and bustle that had preceded our trip. Vangelis returned to his garden and picked two small yellow flowers, handing them over whilst insisting we smelt their fragrance. He then made the *fingers and thumb of the right hand pressed together* gesture whilst extolling the joys of his small garden plot, declaring that no chemicals or pesticides are used. *"Oxi fármaka,"* he declared proudly.

Before we left, I mentioned the incident along the Koula road with the shepherd and his angry dogs. Vangelis listened attentively before confirming that the shepherd was a locally hired Albanian. He also tapped the side of his head, suggesting the guy in question was non-compos-mentis and most certainly unhinged. Then, he offered his advice for the return cycle ride. If the dogs came barking again, we should immediately stop and shout, *"Sta próvata, sta próvata."* These Greek words mean, "go to the sheep, go to the sheep." We said goodbye to Magdalína, thanking her for the coffee, biscuits, and eggs, and then told Vangelis we'd see him again soon at the café in the village square.

On our way back down through Laimos, Claire had a problem with her e-bike. The battery wouldn't switch on. This wasn't an immediate problem, as it was a flat road all the way back to the turnoff for Psarades. But in the rising heat of the morning, it would be impossible for her to cycle all the way up the Devas mountain road without assistance.

We continued to the bottom of the hill, out of Laimos, until we approached the earlier incident spot with the dogs and noticed the flock of sheep was still grazing in the field; their guardian hounds were lying in the shade of a tree. Sure enough, as soon as they spotted us, they stood up and started barking while running in our direction. We stopped cycling, and I began yelling, *"Sta próvata, sta próvata."* Unbelievable but true! Those big, scruffy animals came to a standstill and stopped barking. They turned around and mooched off back in the direction of the sheep. They never bothered us again.

When we reached the turnoff for Psarades, Claire made two brave attempts to tackle the steep road ahead. After running out of pedal power, she resorted to pushing her bike. She got as far as the first of the sixteen sharp bends, then had to stop for a rest. It was pointless trying to continue. It was too steep, too long, too heavy, and too hot to even consider another inch.

It was decided that I'd continue to the village alone and find help or, failing that, return with the camper.

Just as I was preparing to set off on my bike, I noticed, way off in the distance, a white vehicle travelling along the Koula from Laimos. We weren't high enough up the road to see the entire progress, but our fingers were crossed that the vehicle would make the right turn. It was now close to 30 degrees Celsius, and our water supply was dwindling. Then I heard it. The engine sounds of an old pickup truck in high gear coming up the road towards us. Greek farmers call a pickup truck an *agrotikó*. But the English word *truck* is actually from the Greek word *trochós* meaning wheel.

As the small white *agrotikó* approached, I waved frantically to the driver, who stopped just ahead of us. I quickly explained our plight and told him we needed to get to Psarades, where our camper was parked. The word for camper in Greek is *trochóspito*. This word is formed from *trochós*, the word for wheel, and *spíti,* meaning home. Put together, it means a wheeled home. But *trochóspito* originally meant caravan, even though they use it for campers.

The driver and his wife stepped out and helped me lift Claire's bike into the back of the *agrotikó*. I hopped into the back alongside it and held on for dear life as they zoomed off up the mountainside. Claire took command of my fully functioning e-bike and, with full power selected, continued on up the road.

At the entrance to Psarades, it's either straight to the centre of the village or a left turn to the other side of the bay. The driver peered through the small rear window of his *agrotikó* at my wind-lashed face and made another famous Greek hand gesture. It's the one where the right hand is held vertically, and a very swift left-to-right rocking motion ensues. It signifies a question or inquiry. He wanted to know which way to the *trochóspito*. I pointed over to the left, and he roared off in that direction, up the small hill, screeching to a halt just behind the camper in a cloud of dust.

We offloaded Claire's bike, and while thanking him and his wife profusely for their help, I offered a 10 euro note for coffee or drinks. I only wanted to show some appreciation, but it met with a very stark response. *"Oxi, Oxi, Oxi!"* The man almost looked offended at my offer. I tried again, turning to his wife for support, but they were having none of it. I almost got the impression that had I continued to, he might have gotten upset. Instead came another shining example of Greek hospitality towards strangers. Before climbing back into his *agrotikó*, he said, *"We invite you and your wife for coffee at the café of Germanos, okay?"* I agreed to this plan and waved them off.

I grabbed the keys to the battery lock on Claire's bike from the camper. I removed the battery, then refitted it and tried switching it on. It immediately came back to life.

My best guess was that the contacts had become dry and dusty, so a good squirt of electrical contact cleaner cured the problem. Feeling very chuffed with myself, I decided to cycle back to meet Claire, but she suddenly arrived back on my bike at that precise moment.

"Wow! You got it going. Wow, you're a genius! Oh, I'm so happy, thank you, thank you." I didn't know whether to tell the truth, that a simple squirt of cleaning fluid had cured the problem, or dazzle her with some nonsense techno-babble to earn even more brownie points.

So I went for the second option: *"Oh, it wasn't too difficult, love. All I had to do was loosen the grub nuts on the base-plate girdle, then realign the engine mount bushing with a slight readjustment of the phase one regulator, which had disconnected from the battery's dingle arm, resulting in the loss of magneto pulse from the spam-socket."* Claire just rolled her eyes and said, *"So is it fixed or what?"* After explaining the miracle of cleaning fluid, I told her about the invitation for coffee at Germanos's taverna.

Germanos possibly qualifies as one of the oldest residents in Psarades and was born in the village of Agios Germanos, hence his name. He was the first person we met on our first-ever visit to Psarades a few years back and always calls me the "Irish Rover." He can speak excellent English and is also fluent in Hungarian. As it was only our second day back, we hadn't yet called to see him and his wife, but now we had the perfect opportunity.

His taverna is at the far end of the village and is another Greek family-run business. When we got there, he had already heard about the rescue mission with Claire's bike. After exchanging greetings, handshakes, and hugs, he explained that the couple who had helped us were, in fact, his daughter and son-in-law. They were already seated at a table and waving for us to join them.

My happiness hormones were now in full overdrive as I absorbed the present moment in a state of joyful and uplifting blissfulness. It was the beginning of a very euphoric period for us, floating around close to the ether, Zen-like, towards the fourth state of super-consciousness.

Further on, from where we were camped, there is a winding single-track stony path that leads to a headland called Cape Roti. This path dates back to the First World

War and was constructed by French troops stationed in Prespas at that time. It originally served as a military supply route between Florina and Korçë, Albania. From Cape Roti, there are spectacular views across to the Albanian and North Macedonian sides of the lake. In fact, it's so close that our mobile phone networks kept flipping from Greek network providers to those in North Macedonia and Albania.

One early morning, we decided to continue along this path from the Cape Roti turn-off to see how far we could go. It snakes up and through Europe's oldest, largest, and rarest juniper forests. The prickly juniper trees have hard black berries on their branches, emitting a strong gin fragrance. The path narrows after a few miles, eventually becoming overgrown and practically impassable. I estimated that we must have reached a point about 100 metres from Albania. But, of course, there is nothing there to indicate the close proximity to the border.

Most afternoons, I'd cycle down into Psarades to spend an hour or two with another good friend called Kiriaki. She has a small café/store and sells local produce such as honey, assorted varieties of beans, mountain tea and a selection of preserves. Kiriaki and I have a mutually beneficial language agreement. She must speak Greek to me and I'll speak back to her in English. Her café is seldom bustling, so we always have plenty of time for coffee and to right the wrongs of the world. Kiriaki is originally from Kastoria, but her husband, Dimitris, is from Psarades and is well-informed about the area's history.

One afternoon, while we were chatting, he told me about local villages that had simply ceased to exist. Ruins and remnants remain, and, with that in mind, Claire and I set off on our bikes the next day to try and find the remains of these lost villages. I had a small map showing the approximate location of two abandoned villages called Pixos and Daseri.

Pixos once had 350 inhabitants, a school, a church, and a bakery. What on earth could have happened to it? On the map, I could see that it was somewhere east of Vrondero.

Cycling there, we passed by the smaller Prespa Lake and its beautiful island, Agios Achillios. Next came the village of Pili, followed by another steep forested incline.

Just before Vrodero, there is a dirt track off the main road that winds up a hill. Looking at our map, it led to where the ruins of Pixos might be. The track was so steep and stony that we had to push our bikes to the top. Off to our left, I noticed a shepherd with his herd of goats. Straight ahead was a stone building with an old pickup truck parked in front.

As I approached, I saw a huge man loading big, heavy bags onto the back of the truck. He had a shock of black hair and a long dark beard. His left eye socket was closed and completely sealed over, and I noticed that he was missing several fingers on both his left and right hands. When he saw me, he grunted with a wild look in his one good eye. I politely asked, in Greek, if he knew about an abandoned village called Pixos. He just growled, *"What village?"* and returned to lifting his heavy bags. I could tell he was Albanian and had zero interest in us or our quest for the lost village. Then suddenly, from the stone building, a woman appeared, also carrying a big heavy bag, dressed in overalls and a headscarf. She passed the bag to the hairy man and asked me, in Greek, *"What village?"* whilst rotating her right hand in a circular gesture.

I noticed that she was missing every second tooth along the front of her mouth and had hands the size of dinner plates. She hadn't a clue what I was talking about, so I pointed to the trail and asked if we could continue down that way. She shook her head from left to right and then repeated several times, *"Shqipëria, Shqipëria,"* the Albanian word for Albania.

We turned around and headed back down the trail, and as we did, we passed the shepherd with his goats. So I asked him about the whereabouts of Pixos. He was much more helpful and told us it was once near the church further along. Nothing else remained of the village except the restored church, the staircase of an old school, and some scattered foundations of old stone dwellings. And that's all there is of a settlement that was once home to over 350 people.

We were so close to Vrondero that we decided to cycle on and see what was there. The name Vrondero actually means *Thunder,* and the village looks like it has been perpetually subjected to gale-force winds, lightning, hail, tornadoes, and all the dangers associated with fierce thunderstorms. In other words, it looks like a deserted hamlet with very few signs of life.

The road ends here, and Albania is less than a mile further on through thick forest. We thought we might have a coffee or cold drink somewhere, but there wasn't an open taverna or café to be found. Passing one house, I noticed a net curtain twitch, and I could just about make out the silhouette of a spying twitcher in the shadows. We had been spotted. And our presence, no doubt, had been registered. It was a peculiar place, and we both felt it was time to leave.

We later discovered that Vrondero once had a thriving population of about 300 Slavic-speaking Christians. The village was depopulated in 1949, and the Greek State resettled Aromanians, also known as Vlachs, from the Greek regions of Epirus and Thessaly. The Vlachs identified themselves with the Greek nation and culture even though they spoke their own Aromanian language. But why had one ethnic minority been depopulated to make way for a different ethnic group, as was the case in Vrondero? It was becoming increasingly clear to me that this otherwise idyllic region, with spectacular scenery, had a dark and terrible past.

****

The Greek Civil War erupted at the end of World War Two with extreme violence, revenge and human deprivations. An estimated 150,000 Greeks perished between 1946 and 1949 in a devastating conflict that would shatter Greece and transform Europe. This whole area, where we were, was the epicentre of the rebel, or in Greek *antártes,* Greek communist forces.

I knew next to nothing about this conflict until I came here because so little has been documented or published on the subject. It's almost as if it has been forgotten about or overshadowed by other major historical events of the

20th century. It's undoubtedly still a taboo subject in Greece to this day.

The rebel army was finally defeated in 1949 mainly because Britain and the USA supplied the Greek State with an air force. This gave the government forces the upper hand, and they deployed it with deadly effect.

Our old friends in Laimos told us of a night in mid-August 1949, about two months before the Civil War ended, when rebel soldiers ordered many of the villagers to evacuate their homes and march to Psarades.

The villagers protested loudly and told the rebels that they didn't want to leave their homes, but it was to no avail. Taking only what belongings they could carry on their backs or with the use of donkeys and oxen, these unfortunate souls marched out, in pouring rain, across the Koula isthmus towards Psarades accompanied by rebel soldiers carrying heavy weapons and ammunition.

In the skies overhead, seven aircraft of the Greek Air Force appeared. They dived down over the column of evacuees, and by the time it was all over, hundreds of innocent men, women and children lay dead and dying.

These descriptions are very vivid, and they shake me up a lot. We have cycled along this same road many times to drink coffee in Laimos with Vangelis and the others. It's unbearable to imagine what horrors happened here in this otherwise peaceful corner of paradise.

Another story that Vangelis told me was from when he was only 12 years old. Four of his schoolmates had discovered a discarded hand grenade down by the lake. The children started playing with this deadly "toy." When it exploded, it killed three of them and seriously maimed the fourth.

During the Civil War, an estimated 30,000 children were forcibly evacuated from this region by rebel forces to eastern communist states like Hungary, Czechoslovakia, Yugoslavia and Poland. When these children became young adults and tried to return to their homeland, many were refused entry by the Greek State. They were considered *unclean* Greeks, or they were denied citizenship because of their Southern Slavic ethnicity.

Kiriaki told me that Dimitris's father was just a baby when his parents had hidden him from this forced evacuation. His older brother and sister were not so fortunate and were taken away. She told me that the first time her father-in-law ever met his brother was when he was 22 years old, in Berlin, where the brother had finally settled. His sister was 44 when they first met.

In the closing days and weeks of the Civil War, there was a massive exodus of local inhabitants from Prespas to the northern territories of Albania and Yugoslavia. They were in fear of reprisals from the Greek State if they stayed. Once the hostilities had ceased and they tried to return to their homes, they were refused entry. Their homes and farms were confiscated and handed over to Greeks resettled from other parts of the country, such as the Vlachs, now settled in Vrodero. Some deserted villages remained abandoned and were never resettled. Villages such as Pixos and Daseri are such places, and they were either destroyed or fell into ruins.

Our friend Christos, from the taverna *Ta Paragádia* told me about several Civil War bunkers and gun pits used by the rebels at the top of a mountain ridge overlooking Small Prespa and the Koula. On the map, he showed me exactly how to get there by following an almost overgrown trail through the forest of oak and juniper trees. Every 20 metres or so, there is a dirty white cloth marker dangling from a branch. Without following these markers, you would never be able to locate the ruins of the bunkers and probably get very lost.

We cycled to the top of the Devas mountain road one early morning and tied our bikes up behind the small Orthodox Church Ágios Giórgos. We initially got lost but soon found the cloth markers and the trail and proceeded all the way to the top.

What fantastic views awaited us across the Prespa lakes. It was like being offered a beautiful gift just to stand up there and take in the magnificent scenery. The bunkers and gun emplacements are mostly in ruins, but it was nevertheless fascinating to be there and to imagine life for the defenders on the side of the mountain.

One late afternoon, back at the camper, a small car with a Czech registration drove past us and parked nearby. A woman in her late seventies stepped out and stood staring across the bay at the village. I could see that she was upset about something because she was occasionally wiping her eyes. I approached to see what the matter was, and she turned to me and said, *"Over there, in the middle of the village, that was once my school."*

We spoke for a few moments, and she disclosed that she had been an evacuated child. She and her siblings had been sent to communist Czechoslovakia, and this was the first time she had returned to her birthplace in over seven decades.

Our elderly friend Germanos, whose son-in-law had come to our rescue after Claire's e-bike battery problem, had also been sent away as a small boy. He was one of the fortunate ones who managed to return to Greece ten years after the Civil War ended. He had been evacuated to communist Hungary, which is why he can speak fluent Hungarian.

The current population of the Prespa municipality is around 1,200. Seventy years ago, it was close to 7,000. The village of Psarades alone once had a population of over 1,000. These days, it's less than 70. And it's the same story in the other villages and settlements. So it's not only the lakes' water levels that are vanishing from Prespa. The population, too, is in steep decline.

All of this history and nature, the landscapes and vistas, and the local hospitality can mix feelings of joy, happiness and exuberance with a marked melancholy every time I visit here.

After three blissful weeks, we left Psarades and drove south across Central Greece. Before leaving, we had to make one last visit to Laimos on our bikes to say goodbye to the Wise Men of the Village. I lost count of how many times we'd made this 18-mile round trip, but we had certainly made our presence known. Passing cars and trucks would often toot their horns, and outstretched hands would appear from windows, waving with a loud *"Yassas!"* Once, we even got a toot and a big wave from a passing police car.

Before leaving Laimos, I told everyone at the café that we'd do our best to visit again in a few months before leaving Greece for home. Vangelis wished us a *"Kaló Taxídi,"* a good trip, and after embracing us both he spoke in his characteristic soft and gentle manner. *"Never forget, Derek and Claire, the door to my home is always open to you."*

Then he handed me his Greek komboloi, also known as rosary beads or worry beads, as a token of our friendship. I later learned that this is a very meaningful gift in Greek culture and I was very moved by his thoughtfulness. Back in Psarades, we secured all our bits and pieces in the camper, attached the bikes on the back, and drove down the hill to the village to say goodbye to Kiriaki, Dimitris, Eleni, Christos, and the others. More hugs, handshakes, and goodbyes, and finally, we were on our way.

To say I love this corner of Greece would be an absolute understatement. I don't think I could have felt happier during the whole time we were there.

The lockdowns and COVID restrictions during 2020 and 2021 created many dark moments of anxiety and uncertainty for me. But in a tiny Greek fishing village high in the mountains, almost 3,000 feet above sea level, I found myself again—fully repaired and restored.

****

Meteora. Greece's Holy Land

Located next to Kalabaka in northwestern Greece, Meteora is famous for its monasteries built high on immense rock pillars. It would take us about four hours to get there from Psarades, including a stop in Kastoria for food supplies and gas.

At the bottom of the last hill out of Prespas, we turned right, opposite the village of Trigono, and joined the main Florina-Kastoria road. For the next 24 miles, there was hardly any other traffic—just the occasional tractor or *agrotikó*. It felt like we were the only tourists in northwestern Greece.

As we needed to stop for supplies in Kastoria, we pulled over near a supermarket. The carpark was so small we couldn't risk attempting to squeeze in there, so we turned the next corner and, on the opposite side of the street, found a sizeable unpaved area with a few trucks parked up.

It was a dusty place full of potholes, but I found a spot opposite a veterinary clinic. I remember thinking to myself how spick and span this veterinary clinic was, next to a dusty old waste ground. With marbled front steps and a clean, shining shop front, plants adorning either side of the doorway, it looked almost out of place next to a makeshift truck stop.

A few months later into our trip, we would be most grateful for the services of the veterinary surgeon behind the dark-tinted glass of this particular establishment.

While Claire went to the supermarket, I headed into town to find a Pitta Gyros takeaway. It was nearly lunchtime, and this Greek staple was one of our favourite treats.

After the shopping was done and the gas bottles replenished, we motored on to Meteora. We planned to stay two nights, giving us ample time to explore the spectacular landscape and Byzantine Monasteries.

There is a campsite with an outdoor swimming pool in Kastraki, the small village in the heart of Meteora. We arrived there late in the afternoon and got checked in with minimal fuss or COVID bureaucracy. The young mask-less girl at reception was super friendly and invited us to find a camping pitch wherever we wanted. When I asked If the campsite was busy, she looked pretty puzzled, as if I'd just asked the daffiest question ever. *"No, we haven't been busy since summer 2019. There's been a pandemic, you know about it?"* she responded sarcastically.

From the reception area, we drove past the outdoor swimming pool and, around a corner, into a large area with many empty camping pitches. Each pitch was lined with trees, and the whole place looked like a small wild forest. There was a sanitary block at one end for showers, toilets and camper services. With so many choices, finding the ideal location was quite challenging. It was Luxembourg all over again. Eventually, we parked somewhere in the middle, connected to the mains electricity, and settled in.

Away from the mountains, it was much hotter now, with daytime temperatures in the mid to high thirties Celsius. We were feeling pretty grubby from the furnace-like conditions of the day's drive. So that outdoor swimming pool was most definitely beckoning us in. And apart from one young Greek couple playing in the water with their little boy, we had the pool area all to ourselves.

We found a shady corner with a couple of sun loungers, dropped our towels off and plunged into the sparkling, azure pool water. The peaceful, euphoric three weeks we'd just experienced up in Prespas were certainly being fully extended as we bathed in the pool and basked in the soothing tranquillity of our new location. With a panoramic backdrop of steep rocks rising above the surrounding landscape, the pool cooled us down and chilled us out with breathtaking views in every direction.

Back at the camper, Claire prepared dinner, the default spaghetti with chopped vegetables in a pasta sauce, whilst I arranged the table and chairs outside and rolled out the awning. Before bed, we untied the bicycles and prepared them for an early morning start. I wanted to be up and away around 06:30 to get close to the Byzantine Monasteries long before any large coaches packed with tourists arrived.

Meteora is one of the holiest places in Greece. It is derived from the ancient Greek word *Metéoros*, meaning *suspended in the air*. Averaging about 1,000 feet above the ground, the Monasteries look almost like they are clinging to the tops of the giant natural pillars. Monks first settled here in the ninth century to live out their lives in solitude and meditation, which I could relate to after our three weeks in Prespas.

Of the original twenty-four Monasteries, only six survive today and still function as places of religious contemplation and prayer. During Greece's turbulent history, the others were abandoned and fell into ruins, mainly due to thieves, wars, and conquerors.

As planned, we cycled from our campsite at 06:30 all the way to the top. The massive stones are unlike anything we'd ever seen before, and it boggles the mind just how they managed to construct the monasteries in such precarious locations. There are plenty of viewpoints and observation platforms from where you can admire the unique and spectacular landscape.

With no other visitors around at that early hour, I was able to fly my drone and capture some brilliant videos and photos without bothering anyone. By about 09:00, coaches started arriving, and soon, it got busier around the Monasteries. But with the luxury of our e-bikes, we were free to escape the crowds and pedal onto quieter spots.

In fact, we cycled the whole loop around and down to Kalabaka, returning to the campsite just after lunchtime. And just in time, too, as the temperatures started soaring back up to the mid-30s. The afternoon was spent in blissful contentment by the pool with barely another guest to be seen.

Back at the camper, we had neighbours. A small VW van with a Dutch registration had arrived and was parked directly behind us. We couldn't see any sign of life, but I couldn't help but smile at myself. Here in this huge and practically empty campsite, the owners of this van had chosen to park as close as possible to our camper. I wasn't complaining or having any anti-social thoughts; I was merely thinking about how odd it was to park right behind us when there were many other vacant pitches. It was Luxembourg all over again.

We hit the hay early again, as the plan was another cycle trip to the monasteries the following morning. And, sure enough, we were up and away before daylight to complete our early morning mission. With our cameras filled with sunrise photos and our minds etched with unforgettable memories, we returned to the camper for a hearty breakfast before leaving Meteora. There was still no sign of life from the Dutch VW van parked behind us, and I wondered if its owners were alive and kicking.

I sat opposite Claire at our breakfast table with my back to the Dutch van. In between bites of egg on toast, I studied the map for our onward journey that day when Claire gently tapped my plate with a knife. I looked up at her raised eyebrows as she nodded toward the van behind me. I turned my head slowly to witness the rhythmic movement of the small van rocking alternately in a back-and-forth motion. I turned back to Claire and whispered, *"There is life from within."*

That activity, from within, increased profoundly, culminating with an intensity that generated a pronounced squeaking noise from the vehicle's suspension. Then, suddenly, it was all over and seconds later, the sliding door flew open, and a young girl with blonde hair jumped out with a towel wrapped around her torso. *"Goedemorgen!"* she announced with a big, happy, enthusiastic smile. "Good morning!" we answered as she made a beeline towards the shower block.

Moments later, a young guy emerged with a bedraggled bed-head. He looked positively wearied and sapped as he ran his hand through his long, curly locks. *Good Moaning,"* we said simultaneously.

But he was already filled with curiosity at our camper's registration number. *"Waar R U from?"* he asked in a strong Dutch accent, pointing at the unusual alphanumeric characters. So, I gave him the briefest description of the whereabouts of an island in the middle of the Irish Sea. It was obvious to me that the early morning *whoopee* had impacted his attention span, so a full description of the Isle of Man was not crucial.

I was going to mention that his shocks could be worn out or that his rubber spring cups had deteriorated and that liberally applying a good-quality lubricant might quieten the noise. But I didn't bother, as he had already wandered off aimlessly in the direction of the shower block.

After breakfast, we quickly packed up and secured the camper for the road trip ahead of us. From Meteora, we planned to drive via Trikala and Lamia to a coastal village called Paralia Rachon. It's next to the village of Raches on the small Malian Gulf. Just beyond Paralia Rachon is a slither of land that protrudes out into the sea and is very popular with kite surfers. It's also an ideal camper stopover and one that we used eleven years earlier on a trip to Turkey. I'd estimated a journey time of about three hours, which would get us there around lunchtime.

Before leaving the campsite, I popped into the office to say goodbye. The super friendly girl in reception handed me a little packet of sesame seed candy and a tiny wooden frame displaying a Greek Orthodox Icon. It was just a small parting gift, a token of appreciation for our custom. I fixed the religious icon above the entrance door inside the camper with some adhesive. I'm not a religious person, but I am definitely mildly superstitious.

I touched the little icon and wished that our good fortune, positive energy, enthusiasm, and meditative calmness would continue. I wished for many happier times ahead with many unexpected joyful moments.

The road down to Trikala, and further south towards Lamia, was slow going. It was also unbearably hot, with the outside temperature in the low forties. By the time we reached Paralia Rachon, it was mid-afternoon, and all we wanted to do was cool off in the sea.

The slither of land, known as Drepano Beach, was much busier this time around. Because of its windy location, it has become increasingly attractive for kite surfers over the years. It protrudes out into a channel of the Malian Gulf that is directly opposite the most extreme northwestern corner of the Island of Evia. The topography is such that the narrow passage between the mainland and Evia creates a giant Venturi effect, perfect for windy conditions and kite surfing. And they were certainly out in force that day. It was like a free entertainment show watching this exhilarating water sport right before our eyes.

Propelled across the water on small surfboards, this extreme sport is almost like a form of gymnastics. I did wonder how on earth they managed to avoid each other and a mass entanglement of kite lines. But there were no collisions, just a superb display of skill, coordination, and balance that lasted all afternoon.

By evening, Drepano was mostly deserted, apart from a couple of local anglers who had arrived shortly after the departure of the kite surfers. The wind had also dropped dramatically by the late afternoon. From where we were parked, the views across the sea towards Evia were glorious. The colours of the setting sun created a beautiful palette of reds and yellows that deepened and darkened, disappearing into a starry sky. We sat watching the twinkling lights from the coastal villages of the island and contemplated our next move—the Island of Evia.

We had been there once before. That was back in 2019, before the pandemic, but we hadn't fully explored the island. We'd only gone as far as Lefkandi, a beach just south of the island's capital, Chalkida.

Evia is the second largest of all the Greek islands (second to Crete) and is easily accessible by a road bridge between Chalkida and the mainland. Elsewhere, the only access is by small roll-on-roll-off ferries, as there is no airport on the island. From Drepano Beach, the closest port was Glyfa, about 18 miles further east. Before going to bed, I double-checked the ferry times and noted an afternoon departure scheduled for 12:30 a.m. So, leaving around 10:30 in the morning would give us plenty of time to reach the port. After the long, slow, and scorching hot drive from Meteora, we were both ready for an early night.

All alone, parked on the beach, we had a very peaceful and undisturbed rest. It was so peaceful, in fact, that we were wide awake by 05:00. There was excitement in the air. A sense of a new adventure lay ahead with the *Evia Plan*, and we always get very excited and enthusiastic about new adventures.

It was still dark at 05:00, so we made coffee and sat outside, watching the night sky lighten with the rising sun. As we had plenty of time on hand, Claire decided to go for a run, and I prepared my drone to capture some early morning video and photos of the sunrise. At just after 06:00, I launched my *flying camera* and captured the most beautiful sunrise over the Malian Gulf with the corner of northwestern Evia just off to the right. Moments like this, along with the exhilarating sense of freedom and quiet inner joy, stimulate feel-good dopamine hormones into overdrive. Creative ideas flow as a natural consequence of this phenomenon!

During the hour that Claire was away on her morning run, I flew my drone, captured video of the sunrise, transferred the footage to my laptop and edited it into a mini-movie. I also connected my small midi-keyboard to the laptop, where I can access scores of different sampled virtual instruments, and composed a short soundtrack to accompany the video. Usually, I'd have to spend hours piecing together footage and recording sounds for short movies. But that morning, with my endorphin neurotransmitters discharging at peak rate, I had reached an enhanced feeling of well-being and creativity that my mini-project *Sunrise over Evia* took less than 60 minutes to polish off. I was buzzing like a bee in a field of flowers.

After Claire returned from her run, we lazed around on the beach for another couple of hours, as there was still plenty of time before our ferry departed. Then we packed everything away, secured our bikes to the rear, and got on the road to Glyfa.

Getting there was quiet and uneventful, with hardly any other traffic on the road. But all this peace and tranquillity we'd been enjoying since our arrival in Greece was going to be, very suddenly, turned upside down and inside out.

****

Chapter Four

Evia

July 24th 2021

The road that runs down into the tiny port of Glyfa tapers into a narrow street as it reaches the harbour. There isn't much room to manoeuvre in this street, so our concentration levels were elevated, especially with the usual chaotic activity encountered in Greek villages and towns. Keeping an eye out for pedestrians, inching past badly parked cars and delivery vans, not to mention motorcycles weaving in and out of traffic, can quickly fray the nerves. And that particular day was excessively hot, with the temperature soaring above 40 degrees.

As we approached the end of the street leading to the harbour, we saw a lone police officer wearing a black baseball cap, black face mask and black sunglasses. His vest was black, which complimented his black pants, and boots, which were also black. This faceless black uniformed person was waving his arms frantically like the blades of a demented windmill at vehicles on and near the harbour. As soon as he saw us arriving, he started signalling, in a frenzied manner with his spinning arm, towards a corner of the tiny concrete jetty.

As we pulled over, he started yelling, *"ticket, ticket, ticket."* The words sounded like bullets from a machine gun. I got out, and with his arms and hands flapping, he pointed me towards a small wooden office across the street with a sales window and a sign on top with the word *Ticket* displayed. Once again, he fired off the word ticket repeatedly.

As I walked towards the office, he started yelling, *"Mask, mask, mask."* So, I went back to the camper and grabbed a blue face mask. I held it up in the air and waved it at the cop as I walked back towards the ticket office. He nodded his approval, oblivious that I wasn't wearing it, as nobody else was wearing one. This didn't bother the cop in the slightest.

The ticket cost 25 euros for the camper, including two adults. The alternative would have been a 120-mile road trip to the bridge crossing at Chalkida. The ticket sales girl informed me that the ferry was on time and would depart in approximately 25 minutes. Returning towards the camper, I could see the inbound roll-on-roll-off vessel approaching the harbour. As I walked back past the cop, he made that now very familiar gesture to indicate vaccination. It's the thumb up with a pointy finger extended and repeated pokes of the left arm gesture. And, this is where it all went quite crackers.

Poking his arm repeatedly with his pointy finger, he wanted proof of vaccination or a negative rapid test result before we could board the ferry. I told him we had gone through all of these entry procedures to get into Greece, and our COVID-19 PCR tests were now four weeks out of date. *"No, No, No,"* he yelled. *"Must see negative rapid test now."*

The ferry was leaving in less than 25 minutes, so I asked where we could get a test done. He pointed back at the ticket office and fired off *"ticket, ticket, ticket"* again. I ran back over, but there was now a long line of people waiting to buy tickets, so I barged my way to the front and asked the girl at the window, *"Where can I get a rapid test?"* She handed me two forms and said, *"Fill these in, go on the ferry, and you'll be fine." "But what about the actual test?"* I asked her. She stared back at me dispassionately, somewhat dumbfounded and repeated: *"Fill these in, go on the ferry, and you'll be fine."*

So I raced back to the camper, and we filled in the forms, one each with the following requirements:

1. Name
2. Father & Mother's name
3. Date of birth
4. Passport numbers
5. Test date
7. Test results (tick box: negative or positive, your choice!)
6. Signature

I then approached the cop, who didn't bother to check the forms or tickets but started yelling *"ela, ela, ela,"* (come on, come on, come on,) and pointed towards our camper to get moving. Back in the driving seat, I swerved around and headed onto the ferry. There were about 15 crew members, and nobody was wearing high-visibility vests. So, it wasn't easy to distinguish them from all the foot passengers wandering in all directions. And these guys were totally hyper.

There was more *"ela, ela, ela"* and hand waving that was so rapid it appeared blurry. They were running back and forth, then side to side, shouting and directing vehicles into some kind of parking order. They stopped us right in the middle of the deck, causing cars and trucks behind to swerve around us. Then we were directed to the front left-hand side with more highly strung out *"ela, ela, ela"* and blurry hand signals. The vehicles were so tightly packed that it was nigh impossible to exit them and we almost considered getting out of the camper through one of the roof windows.

The crew member, who had just parked the first four lines of vehicles at the front, had effectively sealed himself off from the rest of the ferry, as there wasn't enough room to walk between the parked vehicles. So he jumped up the side of the wall, grabbed a railing and shimmied *Indiana Jones* style across to a suitable landing area.

With our nerves totally frayed, we made our way up the outside stairwell to the passenger deck above when the loudest ship horn in the world suddenly blared in our ears. At this point, I think we both instantly soiled ourselves.

As the ferry left the port, a piercingly loud announcement was made on the ship's public address system. The announcement sounded more like a threat: *"Any passengers who fail to provide proof of vaccination or a negative test and show their identification will be refused access to the vessel."*

But everyone was on the vessel, which was already leaving the harbour. Also, no crew member or official had checked the ridiculous forms we had filled in, our passports, or even our tickets. As the ferry approached Agiokampos in Evia, a classic stampede of passengers ensued down the two adjacent stairwells to return to the vehicle deck. Of course, our camper had been parked right at the bottom of one stairwell, and, one by one, large and small, the stampeding passengers squeezed their way past while I stood by with a bottle of T-Cut 500ml Rapid

Scratch Remover and a rag. The ferry ramp started to lower moments before the vessel actually reached the harbour, and back inside the camper, I sat, ready to start the engine and vacate this floating lunatic asylum.

As I sat there, heartbeat racing and blood pressure soaring, a masked face suddenly appeared at my window and started yelling *"ela, ela, ela"* again with accompanying frantic, blurry hand gestures. We still had the ridiculous forms, our tickets, and our passports to hand just in case they would be checked on arrival. But no such thing happened. Nobody stopped us to question or verify anything. The only visible sign of authority as we descended the ramp was a large uniformed policewoman. She was chain-smoking while chatting merrily with a small group of women waiting to board the return trip to Glyfa. She was completely oblivious to the traffic racing past her from the ferry.

It had been approximately 60 minutes in total time from our arrival in Glyfa to the disembarkation at Agiokampos. It was a short period that could easily have been compared to being incarcerated behind the walls of a secure mental institution for the criminally insane and the warden saying, *"See you in an hour."*

All of the Zen-like calmness and spiritual awareness we had revelled in since arriving in the country four weeks earlier had been shattered in that short space of time.

From Agiokampos, we took a left turn for no particular reason and drove for about 20 minutes without speaking a single word to each other. Such was the trauma of that ferry crossing. We hadn't even made a conscious decision to make that left turn; we just did.

After the 20 minutes of silence, I whimpered to Claire, *"Do you think we should have turned left back there?"* She replied, *"We did turn left. But I don't think it matters that we turned left. We're here now, so let's see where we end up."*

Approaching the town of Istiaia, we spotted a large supermarket, so we stopped to get a few groceries to cover the next few days. I checked on the map to see if there were any small roads leading to beaches and a possible location for the rest of the afternoon and that night, but nothing jumped out at me. It was blisteringly hot, and all we wanted to do was find a quiet corner close to the seaside where we could cool off.

From Istiaia, we continued, passing through the villages of Asmini, Pefki, and Artemisio, but we still didn't find what we were looking for. From Artemisio, the narrow road turns inland, and at a river crossing called Gouva Bridge, road works and a detour took us onto a temporary dirt road. We soon found our way, weaving up and down through heavily forested countryside, seemingly miles from the coast.

I didn't want to say a single word, but I had the impression that we both felt slightly underwhelmed by this corner of the island. In the sweltering afternoon heat, minor disappointments can quickly develop into major frustrations. Further along this forest road, I spotted a water fountain set back from the roadside amongst the trees. We needed to top up our fresh water tank, so I pulled over.

It was a simple open faucet set in decorative granite stone. They are very common in Greece, and people often fill bottles and jerry cans from pure, fresh sources. With two 5-litre water containers, I went to fill the camper's tank only to discover that the water coming from the faucet was a mere trickle. It would take ages to fill up at this rate. So, I returned empty-handed and dejected.

Beneath my feet, the dried leaves, grass, and forest detritus crackled and snapped. The ground was bone dry and dehydrated. The whole area was a tinderbox in the stifling, abnormal heat. It was fair to say that this corner of Greece was suffering from a prolonged and extreme heat wave.

We passed through a village called Agriovotano, and from there, the road descended downhill, in twists and turns, until we reached Ellinika. Just beyond this last village, we saw a narrow road off to our left and turned down it.

There were olive groves on either side of this single track, and it was so narrow the olive branches scraped and scratched down the sides of the camper, leaving me wincing in fear of even more scuffs and grazes to add to all the other scuffs and grazes. Almost instantly, we realised that this left turn was probably not a clever idea. But we had no choice now but to continue. Turning the camper around on such a narrow track was out of the question, and we just hoped there'd be no encounters with traffic in the opposite direction and that we'd find a small beach at the end of it.

Well, there was a small beach, but it was inaccessible. Several cars already occupied the limited parking space, and there was nowhere to turn around. One large lady stood up when she heard our engine and scowled over at us. Not exactly welcoming.

Claire jumped out of the camper to help guide me back to a small field with an open gate. I managed to get turned around there, and we made our way back to the main road unscathed. Before turning onto the main road, we stopped to take stock of our situation. Since boarding that ferry back in Glyfa, our day seemed to have been in a downward spiral. It was now approaching late afternoon, and it was still extremely hot.

We checked our map and saw another village ahead, by the seaside, called Psaropouli. We decided to drive straight there, try it out, and if it proved futile, then we'd call it a day, follow the main road and stop at the next car park, anywhere.

Turning back onto the main road, we continued for about 500 metres when I saw another turn-off to the left. A voice in my head said, *"Ignore it and stick to the plan,"* followed by a second voice saying, *"Go for it; you've got nothing to lose."* I listened to the second voice and made the turn. Claire looked at me confused, *"I thought we were going directly to Psaropouli?"* She was right, but I had a hunch, a feeling in my bones, that this left turn would turn out well. We needed a happy ending to our day.

The winding single track we now found ourselves on wasn't much different from the previous one. Olive trees lined both sides, and their branches clawed at our camper as we passed. That first voice in my head was now mocking the second one. *"Oh dear! Another wrong turn?"* The second voice encouraged me to continue on. *"Fantastic decision, it's going to be magnificent."*

Over a tiny hill and down the other side, I could see waves crashing onto a beach ahead of us. At the end of the track was a sharp turn to the left, and there it was! A beautiful, slightly crescent-shaped beach, about 500 metres long.

Off to our right-hand side was a rock face that jutted out to sea. The road from here ran parallel to the shore and was wide enough for two vehicles to squeeze past each other. *"Wow!"* we both exclaimed in unison. *"This is amazing!"*

Just ahead of us was a wooden changing hut and a shower to the side of it. I jumped out and ran over to check if it worked. I turned the handle, and freshwater gushed out, splashing all over me. I performed a silly little dance of joy while getting completely drenched under the cascading water. On the other side of the changing hut was a wooden bench, and a few metres further on, I noticed a flat grassy area by the roadside. It was a perfect place for us to spend the night.

I ran back to the camper, unable to contain my excitement at such a remarkable discovery. We drove past the grassy area, made a three-point turn on the road, and returned with the camper now facing in the opposite direction. This put the camper's habitation door on the beach side facing the sea. Once we were parked up, I couldn't wait a moment longer. The blue sea with crashing waves was too much to resist. I ran straight in, stopping only briefly to kick off my sandals. What a feeling it was to plunge straight into those waves. All the grime, sweat and frustrations of the day were rinsed away with that single plunge.

I swam out for a few metres before facing in the opposite direction. Off to my left, from where we'd arrived, I could see a small car parked next to several large green rubbish bins. Not far from the car, a single parasol was fixed in the sand and fluttered in the gentle breeze, and in its shade sat a young couple. To my right, the rest of the beach was empty. There wasn't another soul in sight. Beyond the road, I noticed several gated properties set back about 200 metres. Most likely holiday homes for wealthy Athenians. But they all looked unoccupied with their shutters and gates shut. There were no shops, tavernas, or kiosks to be seen anywhere, only a backdrop of high, tree-covered hills and olive groves.

I swam back and, after showering off, returned to the camper. Claire had already arranged the chairs and table outside and was happily doing her crochet. *"Did you enjoy that?"* she asked. *"Amazing! And guess what? We are practically the only ones here."* After our long, wearying day, this was truly the happy ending we had wished for. I encouraged Claire to leave her crochet and join me for another splash before dinner.

As we bobbed around in the waves, I felt a rush of blissful contentment as my Zen returned. On our swim back to shore, I noticed the couple under the parasol had packed up, and the small car was gone. Walking, hand in hand, back to the camper, I turned to Claire and said, *"Can you believe we are all alone in this beautiful place?"* Sweeping my other outstretched hand towards the length of the beach, I continued, *"Just look, there's not a sign of life anywhere."* But I would soon be proven very wrong.

For dinner, Claire boiled up some small potatoes, fried off thinly cut slices of salami and added them to a mixed salad. Simple grub, but very tasty. The afternoon heat dissipated, and the sun sank lower towards the horizon. It was about 7:30 p.m., and in another hour or so, we'd be treated to a spectacular sunset from our peaceful corner of Evia.

Just outside the camper, Claire continued with her crochet while I wrote about the day's events in my diary. I also planned a short post, with photos, for our Facebook travel page, Rocking Life on the Road.

Sitting opposite Claire, I noticed her looking up curiously over my shoulder. *"What's up?"* I asked. *"Oh, it's nothing. I just saw an elderly man walking past,"* she said, *"but something was jumping alongside his feet."* I got up and looked ahead to see the man emerge from the front side of the camper, continuing his short walk towards the end of the road. *"There's nothing at his feet. What did you see?"* I asked.

I had no sooner spoken these words when a tiny kitten emerged from beneath the camper. *"That's it! That's what I saw,"* shrieked Claire. The kitten strolled around our table, then towards Claire and began playing at her feet. She lifted him, and he was completely at ease in her arms. *"My goodness, look how small he is,"* she said. But all I could notice were two big ears sticking up from a tiny head and large front paws that looked utterly out of proportion to the rest of his little body. He also had the cheekiest face, oozing with confidence, and appeared totally unafraid in our company. She placed him gently back on the ground, and he immediately raced over to my side of the table to attack my hand and jiggling fingers. *"He's certainly full of beans. But where on earth did he come from?"*

In the meantime, the elderly man had turned to walk back and was now resting on the wooden bench. I went over and asked him if he knew anything about the small kitten that was now on top of our table, ambushing Claire's crochet wool. The old Greek explained that he was staying at one of the houses further along and that the kitten had appeared from nowhere about 100 metres from our camper. *"Nomízo óti thélei na fáei"* (I think he wants to eat) he added. I asked Claire if we had any of the salami sausage left. She disappeared inside the camper and returned moments later with some finely chopped-up salami meat. The kitten devoured it all before returning to maul Claire's wool. *"Kai neró, prépei na dipsáei,"* (and water, he must be thirsty,) said the man.

I went inside and filled a cereal bowl with water, and sure enough, the little kitten lapped up the entire contents. *"Wow, he must have been dying of thirst; he's drank the whole bowl,"* Claire said.

I returned to the elderly Greek who was steadying himself for his short stroll back to where he was staying. *"And you know nothing about this kitten, or who, maybe, might own him?"* I asked. *"Típota, den écho idéa,"* (nothing, I've no idea,) he replied before changing the subject entirely to tell me all about the next village, Psaropouli. If we needed any supplies, several small mini-markets were open daily in Psaropouli, along with some nice tavernas. I thanked him, but I wasn't the least bit interested in this information. We had no intention of moving from this gorgeous spot; anyway, we had a little guest to entertain now.

"Kaló vrády paidiá!" (good evening, guys!), he said before continuing his gentle stroll back along the road. I turned and went back to Claire, who was having the time of her life with our furry little visitor. The evening sky was now slowly turning a deep red and orange, with the sun seemingly melting into the horizon. I went inside to retrieve a bottle of wine and two glasses. A little

celebration was in order to toast our good fortune in finding such a tranquil place to stay and to honour our little guest.

As I stepped inside, the kitten turned to follow me. The first hurdle was the outside step. With front paws gripping the edge, he tried to pull himself up with both hind legs wind-milling underneath. Claire gave him a little help up, and from there, it was another short pull and push to get to the inside foot well. From there, it was another grapple to reach the inside of the camper. Once inside he looked to his left, then right, before sauntering up to the cab area. *"What's he up to?"* Claire asked. *"Well, you're not going to believe this. He's just pulled himself up onto the driving seat, has curled up and is now nodding off."*

Outside, the sunset was now in its full fiery glory. I poured our wines and sat staring out across the small bay. *"Gosh! What a day it's been,"* I said. Claire smiled back and whispered, *"Yes, it has, but what are we going to do about him?"* nodding towards the camper. We didn't ponder this for too long. It was quite clear to both of us that the kitten was exhausted and that there was no way he could stay outside overnight. He was now flat out on the driving seat, fast asleep and safe and sound.

We'd wait until morning and then ask around. Somebody must know something, and if not, then we'd figure something else out. For now, at this precise moment in time, nothing else seemed to matter. We were all alone on this quiet beach, happy, safe and content, just the three of us. A gentle, warm evening breeze softly swirled across the beach; the sea had mellowed out, and small waves now lapped the shoreline. Straight ahead, the sun slipped behind the horizon. It was the end of one day's journey and the beginning of a new adventure in the morning. As the sun disappeared below the horizon, the long day finally caught up with us, too. We were fast asleep by 9:00 p.m. and didn't wake up all night.

Around 06:30, I was stirred from my slumber by a squeaking sound, a trilling noise from just below our bed. I glanced down, still half awake, and in the dim light, I could make out a little pair of beady eyes staring back up at me.

No, it wasn't a dream. There was a kitten in our camper. I quickly gathered my thoughts as the events of the previous evening finally dawned on me. Our bed is positioned from left to right, at the back, and the distance from the floor to the top of the mattress is almost one metre high. The kitten started jumping up the side in an attempt to reach the bed, but it was a lost cause. It was just too high up for him.

Now fully awake, I swung out of bed and slipped on my sandals. The kitten raced ahead of me and jumped onto the inside step by the habitation door. He wanted to go outside. So I opened the door, and he immediately jumped onto the outdoor step and from there to the ground, landing awkwardly on the sand and pebbles. A little shaken but not stirred, he darted off to just beyond the camper and started digging a hole in the ground.

I sat on the step and observed what seemed like a major excavation as he hollowed out a pit approximately the size of his own body. With the unearthing complete, he lowered himself in and seconds later, job done, climbed back out. A major cover-up followed as he clawed back all the loose sand and earth to fill the crater he had dug out. In between sniffing the ground, he continued the laborious chore for several more minutes until everything was concealed and well camouflaged.

I returned inside to put the kettle on, leaving the kitten to stalk, ambush and pounce on multiple objects lying strewn around outside. *"Where is he?"* yawned a bleary-eyed Claire, sitting on the edge of the bed. I explained how he'd burrowed a hole outside big enough to hide in, all for a little puddle. *"He's certainly very clean then?"* she said. *"Or he's just prone to an extremely intensive hygiene routine?"* I replied while looking outside at him, disembowelling a small piece of driftwood.

Claire made the coffee while I arranged the table and chairs outdoors for our morning brew. The sun was rising above the hills behind us, casting colour and light across the sea and sand. We sat outside sipping our coffees while, beneath the table, tiny nipping teeth and claws targeted our toes and ankles. I chopped up the last of the salami meat and served it up with a bowl of milk. He devoured the meat but wasn't interested in the milk. So I swapped it for water, which he gulped down. Then he sauntered over to the step, pulled himself up, and climbed inside. I waited a few moments before checking to see what he was doing. He'd settled back on the driver's seat again, as bold as brass, and had proceeded to groom himself before an early morning snooze.

I decided to go for a swim prior to conducting a full investigation into the enigmatic kitty. It was Sunday morning, and several families and young couples were already arriving to stake their claim to a piece of beach for the day. After my morning dip, I went off on my bicycle to see if I could find any clues that would solve the mystery. And that's exactly what it was: a mystery.

I cycled the entire length of the beach road, paying careful attention to gaps in the hedges, gateways to private homes, clumps of grass, trees, and anything that might reveal or conceal a mother cat with kittens or just other kittens. But there was nothing.

On the way back, I stopped to ask a woman out on her morning stroll. She told me she was staying in the nearby village Agios Nikolaos but couldn't offer any help or clues. She mentioned that stray and abandoned dogs were occasionally found on the beach, but she had never seen any cats.

The holiday homes closest to us were unoccupied, fenced off, and secured with closed gates. The fences were chain-link with gaps too narrow for a kitten to squeeze through. I returned to the camper to find Claire busy with her crochet while fending off an inquisitive kitten who was giving her wool his full and undivided attention.

The place was starting to get busy now, with more young families, pensioners, and teens arriving. Little Greek kids were running in and out of the water, shrieking with joy, while young dudes played bat and ball games. Elderly Greeks bobbed up and down in the water in circles, chatting so loud their conversations could be heard halfway down the beach. It was a classic *Greek day at the beach* scene.

We didn't know it then, but amongst this colourful and happy activity was a lovely couple on holiday from Athens. They had noticed our camper and were interested in the registration number. It would be another twelve months before we'd actually meet them and kindle a very close friendship.

It was approaching mid-morning, and the temperature was already sky-high. The day before, it had reached almost 40 degrees Celsius by mid-afternoon, and the best place to be, maybe the only place to be, was by the sea. After rolling out the camper's awning, I took a short walk to the end of the beach, where the rocks jutted out to the sea. A small path continued up past the large green rubbish bins, and I continued hoping to see or hear a mother cat with her kittens. But there was nothing, and even if there had been, they would have been curled up, sleeping somewhere in the shade, trying to stay cool. And on the subject of staying cool, it was high time I found some shade.

Claire had made a big salad with Feta cheese, and we enjoyed an early lunch while contemplating our next move. The kitten had decided it was too hot outdoors and had discovered probably the coolest place indoors.

Next to the fridge, there's a narrow storage space for our foldaway table. It's just big enough to accommodate the table and nothing more. Well, that's what we thought until the kitten climbed in there to enjoy this cool, dark space. I had nothing left to feed our furry guest. It was also a Sunday, and finding a store that was open could prove difficult. We waited another couple of hours, had a few more swims, and then decided to move on.

As far as the kitten was concerned, the decision to take him with us had become a foregone conclusion. We simply could not have left him behind. The heat alone would have dehydrated his little body, and without shelter or sustenance, I doubt he would have survived another 24 hours on his own. And so it was that this tiny fur ball, with big ears and giant paws, scooped a free ride off the beach and onto one of many new adventures.

We'd both agreed that travelling with a pet was not something we had planned, and our next best option was finding him a caring home. Surely someone, somewhere, would like to adopt this little guy or girl? We'd been referring to the kitty as he/him since the previous evening when the truth was that neither of us was sure. At only a few weeks old, it's difficult to figure out a kitten's gender. I'd even checked online to discover the following words:

Sexing kittens under eight weeks of age is even more difficult because the structures you are looking at are tiny and relatively underdeveloped.

Claire had already decided it was a boy as, and I quote, *"He's just such too cheeky and feisty. No way a girl would carry on like that."*

Before leaving, we ran through the usual routine of securing all loose objects inside, closing cupboard doors, securing locks, and checking that the bikes were securely attached to the bike rack. Seated inside and buckled up, Claire took the kitten in her arms as I started the engine. We both expected him to freak out at the noise, but he wasn't in the slightest bit bothered. He simply turned his head slightly to one side as I put the camper into gear, and we moved off. Then, within seconds, he was fast asleep on Claire's lap.

At the main road, I took a left turn, and we continued up a steep hill, passing the road junction for Psaropouli. I glanced at Claire's lap and thought to myself how different the past 24 hours could have been for us and this snoozing fur ball. If I hadn't made that turn the day before and continued on as planned to Psaropouli, none of this would have happened.

After only four or five miles, we passed through a village called Vasilika. On the right side, there was a mini-market open for business. I managed to pull over a short distance further on and walk back to the store where they stocked pet food. So I bought a few tins and a small plastic bowl and returned to the camper to serve lunch. And it went down a treat. As he scoffed half a tin of cat food, I realised that what goes in has to come back out later, and we didn't have a litter tray.

Back at the store, I tried to explain what I needed. I had no idea how to say *"litter tray"* in Greek, so I tried words like *"toilet for cats."* After a quick glance around, I returned to the camper empty-handed. *"We'll just have to keep an eye on him. And if he needs to go, well, we'll pull over,"* Claire said. *"Easier said than done on these narrow roads,"* I replied.

We continued south, passing a settlement called Strofilia. It was far too hot to stay inland, and it would take us another two hours, at least, to reach Evia's capital, Chalkida. So we looked at the map and decided to head west to a place called Limni. Just beyond this small coastal town, we found a secluded beach called Koxyli, where we could stop for the night. There were no showers, shops, or facilities nearby, but it was fine for a stopover, and we had everything we needed anyway. The kitten was keen to get outside and check out the new surroundings, never straying too far from us.

After cooling off in the sea, we relaxed for the entire rest of the afternoon under the shade of our awning.

There was nobody else around until late afternoon when a car pulled up with four kids in the back.

The Mum and Dad set up a mini-camp nearby with a large parasol, chairs, towels, a cooler box and bags of snacks. The kids, aged between four and ten, raced off to the water's edge with their fishing nets, buckets, and spades.

The youngest child was a little girl, and now and then, she'd glance over in our direction with a puzzled look on her face. *"I'll bet you it's not the registration number that's grabbed her attention,"* I quipped. She then ran back to her parent's side and whispered something in her Mum's ear while pointing at us. The parents smiled and gave us a little wave.

Then, the little girl walked straight towards us and pointed to the kitten playing at our feet. *"Pós ton léne to gatáki?"* she asked me. She wanted to know the kitten's name, and I didn't know what to tell her. I glanced at Claire, then at the *gatáki,* running and chasing after a discarded wrapper, and then back at the little girl. She continued to stare at me, waiting patiently for a name. I glanced once again at the ground and at the kitten, with a plastic wrapper now dangling from his mouth. It hadn't yet occurred to us to give him a name. Then it struck me out of the blue

I looked up and smiled at this curious child and told her, *"Vangélis. To ónomá tou eínai o Vangélis"* (Vangelis. His name is Vangelis.) With that, she ran off towards her brothers, whooping with joy, *"Vangelis! Vangelis! His name is Vangelis!"* And the most remarkable thing was that the newly christened Vangelis scampered off after her.

He stayed with the kids for the entire afternoon, jumping in and out of the holes they'd been digging in the sand and attacking their fishing nets. One of the boys had filled a bucket with seawater to empty into a moat he'd dug around his sandcastle. But Vangelis kept getting in the way and wouldn't budge from the moat much to the amusement of the children and their parents looking on.

Late afternoon, the family started packing their things and got ready to leave. The little girl ran over to us and asked if Vangelis would be back tomorrow. I felt a twinge of disappointment telling her he might not be because we had to travel somewhere else but that he'd had so much fun playing with her and her three brothers.

As she ran back to her parents, I almost considered asking them if they would like to adopt the kitten. After all, that was the plan, to re-home him, to find him a safe place where he'd be well cared for and loved. But I didn't ask, or I couldn't ask, not just yet anyway.

The following morning, we set off bright and early for Chalkida. All stores and businesses were open again after the weekend, and our first stop was at a large pet store we found called *Pet City* on the main road into the Chalkida. We stocked up with wet and dry kitten food, a cat's scratching pole, a litter tray and a couple of bags of cat litter. Vangelis had been doing his business outdoors, but having the tray would be very useful if we were on the move and he had to go. We also bought a couple of kitten toys in the hope that they would divert his playful interest away from our toes and ankles.

From Chalkida, it's a short drive south to Vasiliko, where there's a nice beach called Paraliakí Poseidónos with ample parking not far from the town. We'd already

113

visited this place two years earlier, so it was all very familiar. A line of small trees offer shade between the parking area and the sandy beach. There's a freshwater shower between these trees and a public toilet about half a mile back. The lively seaside town of Lefkandi is only a mile and a half further along and has plenty of tavernas, cafés, shops and bars.

But for us, the small tree-lined beach was an idyllic and peaceful location for a few days. The sand was hard and compacted, so I manoeuvred the camper from the parking area and onto the beach. The mainland is only two miles, or less, across the South Evian Gulf, and the channel between creates another top location for kites and windsurfers.

It's also a magnet for sea anglers. They arrive very early in the morning, before daylight, and set up their fishing rods, parasols and paraphernalia. It can get quite crowded as they converge in the same spot, many with multiple fishing rods firmly anchored to the beach.

By the time we arrived, it was mid-morning, and they were already dispersing because of the strong sun and heat. We let Vangelis out as soon as we were settled, and he went straight up a tree. This would prove to be one of his favourite activities, that and lurking in the long grass. There was also plenty of shrubbery around the base of the trees, which was another favourite hiding place. Pensioners, who arrived early every morning for a swim and a gossip, had also packed up and left and we were soon by ourselves.

By late afternoon, the place got busy again with young families and elderly folks arriving to escape the infernal heat of the day and enjoy a cool dip in the sea.

The anglers also returned with their rigs and settled in for another afternoon and evening of shore fishing. This activity soon caught the attention of a very inquisitive kitty. The fishing lines, shiny spinners, lures and nets must have been too much to resist. We didn't actually notice he'd gone until Claire spotted a tiny object racing back towards the camper from the direction of the anglers. It was Vangelis, and he had a tiny sprat in his mouth. It was obviously a gift from one of the guys fishing, and it was now being offered to us. He dropped the fish inside the camper and then headed back in the direction he'd come from.

I followed him to make sure he wasn't causing any trouble. The guys weren't bothered in the least; in fact, they were more curious as to how and why a kitten had barged into their fishing hotspot. They were also very amused by the name I had given him. I also began telling them all about the events of the past couple of days whilst Vangelis raced up and down after shoals of tiny fish close to the shore. It was the sun glinting off the fish that had attracted him, but every time he got close to the water, his paws would get soaking wet, and he'd retreat to dryer ground.

I wished everyone a *"kalispéra,"* grabbed Vangelis and walked back to the camper. There were more visitors now, and the numerous cars passing by worried us a lot.

As long as Vangelis stayed on the beachside of the road behind the tree line, he'd be safe, but if he started wandering around the parked cars, or worse, onto the road? I shuddered at the thought and made a mental note to buy a small harness and rope the next time we were at the shops. We might have to tether him when parked up at busy places.

Over the next few days, we settled into our usual relaxed and laid-back routine of early morning walks and afternoon swims. I also realised it had been several days since my last post on our Facebook travel page. In fact, the last thing I'd written about was the Glyfa ferry trauma.

That evening, I sat down and introduced Vangelis to our online friends and followers, explaining how he'd appeared from nowhere, taken over, and was now travelling in luxury. I included photos of the scruffy little dude with huge ears and oversized paws with my story and hit the post button.

I was absolutely astonished when I checked our Facebook page the following morning. Normally, our travel blogs reach several hundred people and garner about 20 or 30 reactions, along with a few comments.

However, the story about Vangelis already had over 10,000 reaches. There were dozens of heartfelt comments, and the reactions weren't just *likes.* They were mainly *loves* and *cares.* Claire also noticed that the number of followers on the page had increased by several hundred, and the post had been shared 75 times.

I also noticed that many of the well-wishers were from distant places like Canada, South Africa, Australia and the United States.

I spent an entire morning reacting to and replying to all the comments. A recurring theme throughout, expressed in the heart-warming comments, was one of joy and uplifting happiness:

"This has really made my day! Hugs from a locked-down Melbourne."

"This has made me smile from ear to ear."

"A wonderful story, and it looks like he's chosen you!"

"This has cheered me up no end."

"OMG, that made me well up."

And this was just within the first 12 hours. Looking back on that first story about the "abandoned kitten", the total number of people it reached was over 83,000. Subsequent posts would top over 100,000. I now had a full time job telling the world about the adventures of Vangelis.

Two days later, I wrote my next Facebook post about his tree-climbing skills and his friendly encounters with the local fishermen. I also wrote about Greek *filoxenia* (Φιλοξενία), meaning hospitality, and a Greek lady called Yana. *Filoxenia* comprises two words: *filo*, meaning friend, and *xenia*, meaning foreigner or stranger. So it's like saying friendship to a stranger.

Every morning and late afternoon, a small white Suzuki jeep pulled up nearby. A lady in her early seventies stepped out, arranged a lounge bed in the shade, and read her book. She had two small dogs with her who occasionally came sniffing around our camper, much to the vexation of Vangelis. One afternoon, she approached me and said, *"Excuse me. Do you know where that little kitten is?"* I smiled and pointed at the camper. *"He's inside at the moment, in the coolest place he can find."* Quite surprised, she answered, *"Oh, he's yours?"* Then, she produced several small packets of kitten food and biscuits from the back of her jeep. *"Here, this is for your kitten."*

She had seen Vangelis playing up in the trees on her previous visits to the beach and assumed that he had been abandoned there. She had brought the cat food to feed him, not realising that he had already travelled from the other side of Evia inside our camper and was fast becoming a famous internet celebrity.

As the sun started to set, this charming lady packed away her things and waved goodbye, saying, *"Ta léme ávrio,"* meaning *"see you tomorrow."* However, about three hours later, while we were sitting outside in the cooler night air, she came back with a big bag of oranges from her own orange grove and 12 eggs from her chickens! There must have been at least four kilos of oranges in that bag. And this *filoxenia* is what we encounter everywhere we travel in Greece.

It doesn't matter if it's a small bag of tomatoes from an elderly Greek man's garden or some homemade biscuits from his wife; it's not actually the gifts; it's the fact that they do this with such care, thought, and consideration. I've probably written a hundred times about these small random acts of kindness from one stranger to another and how this can truly overwhelm us sometimes.

The daily news reported from the rest of Europe and around the world is rarely good. It's often hostile, worrying, confusing, angry, and very uncertain. Politics and fear are so divisive and corrosive. This toxic mix can divide and separate us. And that is not how it should be because we're all very capable of a little *filoxenia.*

Yana called every morning and afternoon to swim and relax on her lounge bed in the shade. It was an excellent opportunity for me to practise my Greek, as she didn't speak any English. She always brought a small packet of treats for Vangelis, who was, by now, starting to tolerate her two small dogs.

One afternoon, she asked me what we planned to do with him. I told her that we had never intended to travel with a pet and that we'd only taken him with us because he would not have survived otherwise. I could see that Yana was fond of him, so I asked if she would like to adopt him. Even asking this question was hard as we were still in two minds. But the decision to give him up would have been easier if we were certain he would be cared for. Yana explained that, as much as she would like to, it wasn't an option because of her two dogs. She also added that it might prove difficult, in Greece, for us to find a home for him.

Another friendly visitor to the beach was a guy called Stefanos. He had lived and worked all his life in Athens but was now retired, living in a nearby cottage with his wife. They had a huge garden where he grew many fruits and vegetables. One morning, he appeared outside our camper with four large plastic bags stuffed with leafy greens. It was Greek *horta* from his garden. He instructed Claire and me to fetch basins and buckets of water into which he plunged the leafy green produce. *Horta* literally means *weeds,* but it looked more like spinach or kale in this case. In fact, the Greek word for vegetarian is *hortofágos*, which literally means *weed eater.*

Stefanos carefully washed the *horta*, leaf by leaf, before tossing them into a colander. Endless chatter accompanied every wash and rinse as he kept assuring us of how delicious it would taste.

I learned a new word that morning: *Zouzoúnia*. It means bugs or tiny insects, and he kept repeating this word over and over, paying careful attention in case there were any *zouzoúnia* crawling around in the *horta*.

After washing and rinsing were completed, he instructed Claire in fine detail on how to cook and serve this classic Greek dish. A drizzle of olive oil and lemon juice was absolutely essential, as was a pinch of salt and pepper. Chopped garlic was optional. That evening, we feasted on plates of *horta* with crusty home-baked bread, and it was indeed delicious!

Stefanos was a member of the group of pensioners who arrived every morning for a noisy get-together, bobbing around in the sea. If you can't see Greeks near you, you will definitely hear them.

Once he'd got to know us, he visited daily, always bringing a small gift like olives, fruit, feta cheese, and even once a bottle of olive oil.

By the beginning of August, we were still on Evia, at the same spot, when I wrote up another story about Vangelis. It was to thank everyone who had shown such an interest in him and to bring everyone up to date on his antics and global popularity.

He'd only been with us for over a week, and in that short time, he'd touched the hearts of tens of thousands of people from all over the world. It was really astonishing just how popular my Facebook posts had become since he showed up:

"Makes my heart soar when I see a new post!"

"An amazing get-together; some things are just meant to be."

"He is a gift from the gods!"

"I beg you, don't leave him."

"Love your posts about Vangelis; they always bring happiness."

It became clear to us that the stories about this little kitten impacted many people very positively. All over the world, people endured hardships with the pandemic and the consequences of lockdowns, restrictions, and loss of freedoms. And it wasn't even over yet. Many countries were still in lockdown, and governments continued to enforce draconian measures on their citizens. Uncertainty and fear were still prevalent.

Families who wanted to travel or have a holiday chose not to because of the perceived dangers and difficulties involved. *Stay-cation* became the new buzzword for stay-at-home holidays.

The story of the abandoned kitten radiated a genuine feel-good effect in contrast to the doom and gloom of the previous 18 months. This was definitely alluded to in the hundreds of comments that followed my posts.

The day before we left Evia, the wind picked up considerably, and from about mid-afternoon, there was increased activity from dozens of kite surfers and windsurfers. The small car park was packed with vehicles as more enthusiasts arrived with their colourful kites and sails.

From the beach, we watched on and were treated to a spectacular display of aerobics, speed, and skills. Vangelis had been in his cool place inside the camper, but when I checked on him, he was nowhere to be seen. We looked up the trees and around the camper, but there was no sign of him. Claire looked along the beach while I checked the car park. A group of kite surfer dudes had gathered beside their cars and were chatting away when I passed by, looking for and calling out Vangelis's name. Two of the guys swung around and said, *"Nai?"* (Yes?)

They were also called Vangelis and were clearly wondering what I wanted from them. I explained that we had a kitten by that name, but he'd gone missing.

Then I heard a voice from the next vehicle asking in English, *"Hello, is this what you are looking for?"* It was a young Greek guy standing alone in front of his car's open boot. I went over, and inside the boot was a very curious kitty. We laughed about it, but it had been a very close call. The guy was on holiday and had been out windsurfing all afternoon. He'd just finished packing his things and was about to shut the boot and drive off. We stood and chatted for a moment while Vangelis writhed in my arms. He worked in Brussels as an I.T. specialist but visited his family on Evia every summer. He was very interested in our visit to his home island and the whereabouts of the Isle of Man. He'd spotted the unusual registration on the camper and was intrigued by it, never having seen a Manx registration before.

The wriggling and writhing ball of fur I was cradling also intrigued him, so I gave the short version of events. We then wished each other a good evening, and I hastily returned to the camper just in time to meet Claire, who was returning from her own search and rescue mission.

She smiled, with evident relief, at the sight of Vangelis again. *"So where was he?"* she asked. *"In the back of a windsurfer's car boot,"* I replied, *"and luckily for him and us, he was spotted; otherwise, he'd have been gone for good."*

Claire took him from my grasp and gave him a big hug, followed by a kiss on the head. It wouldn't be the last time we'd temporarily lose this curious, mischievous kitten, nor the last time we'd lose our minds with worry.

The following morning, we decided to move on from Poseidónos beach and head west towards another of our treasured locations: the seaside settlement of Krioneri, about 24 miles further west of Nafpaktos.

Our original plan was to visit our friends in Loutsa, a town on the Aegean Sea coast just east of Athens. I've known "Nick the Greek" and his English wife Helen for over 30 years. In fact, 2020 should have been our year for a big celebration, marking 30 years of friendship, but the pandemic got in the way.

We had to reshuffle our plans again because it was too hot to go anywhere near Athens or the suburbs. By 10:00 in the morning, the mercury was hitting 40 degrees Celsius in the shade. We couldn't have left Vangelis locked inside the camper, and we couldn't have brought him indoors because of their big, crazy dog, Molly. So we decided that we would arrange to meet up somewhere else before we left Greece.

I didn't want to leave the beach without first saying goodbye to our lovely friend Yana. She had visited every day for her swims and relaxation. She had also kept Vangelis constantly supplied with treats and toys.

Sure enough, she arrived in her white Suzuki jeep around 10:00. Once parked under the shade of the trees, she approached me with a large red plastic box in her hand. It was a pet carrier! She handed it over, saying, *"It's a bit old, and one of the door's hinges is broken, but maybe you can fix it? Anyway, you can keep it in case you need to take Vangelis to the vet."*

Once again, I was very grateful and genuinely touched by this kindly Greek lady's *filoxenia*. Strangely enough, getting a pet carrier for Vangelis was on my shopping list at the next available opportunity. However, Yana's thoughtfulness pipped me to the post. Was it just a coincidence, or was she psychic or telepathic? Either way, I filed this occurrence of serendipity under the abstract theory of Greek metaphysics.

I chatted with Yana for a while and told her our intentions to travel to Western Greece later that morning.

Then, out of the blue, she asked, *"You gave him the name Vangelis?"* Quickly followed by, *"Why this name? Do you understand what this name means?"* I told her I had no idea what it meant, that it was just a name I'd come up with while being interrogated by a little Greek girl on a beach in Limni.

Yana continued to explain that Vangelis derives from the Ancient Greek words ευ, meaning good, and άγγελμα, meaning messenger or bearer of good news, which combine to mean: *Messenger of Good News.*

I was honestly dumbfounded. Over the past week, that is exactly what this kitten had become. The posts on our travel page had gone viral and reached many thousands of people all over the world. This little kitten's survival tale touched and endeared everyone who followed it. The comments, reactions, and positive feedback were all testaments to a very faithful *Messenger of Good News.* A true Vangelis!

I then recited word for word, the meaning of the Greek words ευ compounded with άγγελμα over and over in my head. I was starting to accept, without question, Philosopher Aristotle's belief that *"everything happens for a purpose."*

After packing everything away and securing the camper, we went over to say goodbye. Yana smiled, hugged us both, and then wished us a *"Kaló taxídi"* safe journey.

I thanked her for all the oranges and eggs, the toys and treats for Vangelis and, of course, the red pet carrier with the broken hinge. I also told her we would return to Evia and Poseidónos beach before leaving Greece. *"So we'll meet again,"* she said with a sincere smile. And with that, we were on our way.

****

Chapter Five

The Road to Krioneri

From Evia's capital, Chalkida, back to the mainland, there are two connecting bridges: the old bridge and the high bridge. We took the latter and proceeded west across central Greece towards Thiva (Thebes) and on to Livadia. A quicker option to reach Western Greece would have been the highway from the north of Athens to Patras, but it's a less interesting route and it's also an expensive toll road.

We've travelled along the northern Gulf of Corinth many times before to reach Athens, and the beautiful scenery en route makes this longer journey so worthwhile.

From Livadia, the flat landscape gives way to mountainous terrain as the road winds up through pine forests towards Ancient Delphi. We took a shortcut at a junction 15 miles before Delphi, near Distomo, and headed south via Desfina to Itea and then on to the seaside town of Galaxidi. Just two miles beyond Galaxidi, a sharp left turn off the main road leads down a steep hill to a tiny beach called Anemokámpi with a large eucalyptus tree. It's opposite a marine farm and is a perfect location for a stopover.

It was early afternoon when we arrived there, and the heat was, as usual, unbearable. Apart from trying to keep ourselves cooled down, we now had the additional responsibility of our furry little companion. We'd tried soaking tea towels in water, rinsing them off, then placing them in the freezer box. The idea was to create a cool pad for him to lie on, but it didn't work as planned. So next, we froze water in plastic bottles and placed them on the driver's seat once we'd stopped. This idea worked very well. Vangelis would hop up and lean against the bottles, sometimes with an elbow propped up on one, until his little body cooled down. But these measures were only temporary as the inside of the camper was ridiculously hot, even with the windows wide open. We had the luxury of throwing ourselves into the sea to cool off, but this wasn't an option for a tiny kitten.

The only other visitors on the small beach that day were Italians with a caravan. We exchanged waves, hellos and *"ciaos"*, and I could see they were also sweltering in the stifling hot afternoon air.

We rolled out our awning, set up our table and chairs under the shade, and spent the afternoon between the sand and the sea. Around mid-afternoon, I went to check on Vangelis, who had been remarkably quiet since we had arrived. Two plastic bottles of chilled water were inside the camper, on the driver's seat, but there was no sign of him. I checked down around the footwells and at the rear of the camper next to the fridge. Nothing!

Outside, I alerted Claire to his disappearance, and we both set off on a search and rescue mission. She went to ask the Italians if they had seen him whilst I crossed the dusty track we'd driven down to see if he was sleeping in the long grass beyond. But even that didn't make any sense as the grass offered no shade, and the ground's surface was roasting hot. It wouldn't have been comfortable on his little paw pads to walk around in the blazing afternoon sun, either. I went over to the single cucalyptus tree on the beach, hoping that he might be hiding up in the branches, but there was no sign of him.

We both checked under the camper to no avail. Claire returned to the Italians one more time, only to ask if they could check inside their caravan. This really seemed to bother them as they dismissed Claire's request with a *"No gatto! No gatto!"*

By now, his absence was really starting to worry us, and it's typical that in these anxious moments, you start behaving almost irrationally. I began looking inside cupboards and lockers, fully realising that he couldn't possibly have gotten into such places. Claire crawled around on her belly underneath to see if he was sitting on an axle or hiding behind a wheel. We started retracing our moves since arriving, but nothing out of the ordinary had occurred other than simply parking up and going for a swim. Vangelis had been inside on the seat when we stopped, next to his cold water bottles, and now he was gone.

Beyond the small beach, there was an old, derelict hotel with lots of wild dogs roaming around. I shuddered to think that maybe one of those dogs might have got him. But that thought soon disappeared, as it was quite a distance to the baying hounds, and we would have definitely heard something had any of them come close to us. There was nothing else we could do but wait, hoping that he would miraculously return to us.

My thoughts turned to Yana's explanation and the significance of the name Vangelis. I hoped and prayed that this particular *Messenger* would soon bring some *Good News* to his very anxious guardians. In an attempt to distract myself from everything, I glanced at the local and international news online. The main headline was Evia. And it wasn't good news at all.

Wildfires had engulfed vast areas of the island's northern half just days earlier. The heatwave we were experiencing had temperatures hitting over 45 degrees Celsius (113 degrees Fahrenheit). This heat and tinderbox conditions on the ground contributed to the most destructive blazes in the island's recent history.

Over 300,000 acres of forest and arable land were burnt, and about 2,500 people had to be evacuated by ferries. The wildfires had raged through many of the places where we had recently been, and I immediately recognised the names of the villages and settlements affected. Istiaia, Agios Nikolaos, Psaropouli, Vasilika, Agia Anna, and even Limni, the northwestern coastal town where the little Greek girl had asked about the kitten's name.

The size and scale of the destruction was truly harrowing. We would learn later that half of the island of Evia had been burnt. The north, where Vangelis found us, had suffered apocalyptic destruction. The sheer scale of it all was almost too unbearable to imagine.

Vangelis was starving and extremely thirsty when he came to us that evening, only days before the big fires engulfed the region. We were very fortunate indeed. A sense of relief swept over me as I realised how close we had been to that inferno. Miraculously, we had departed the north of Evia just in time and avoided being caught up in the ferocious conflagration. A tiny kitten had also dodged disaster but was now lost once more.

While quietly pondering and mulling over all of these thoughts and events, I heard a tiny squeak from behind me. Claire had clearly heard it, too, because she was staring at me wide-eyed. *"Did you hear that?"* she asked excitedly. Before I could answer her, there was another squeak as we both clambered to our feet and swung around to face the camper. There, just behind the back wheel, was a very sleepy-eyed Vangelis. His eyes rolled back as he let out a big yawn before stretching forward.

We whooped with total joy. *"He hasn't been far,"* said Claire. *"Look, he's just woken up. The wee monkey has been right under our noses this whole time."* She picked him up for a celebratory cuddle whilst I ducked under the camper for clues to Houdini's hiding place.

Positioned left to right, behind the rear axle, is the camper's 100-litre fresh water tank. As I looked up, I could see a small gap between the top of the tank and the rest of the chassis. I crawled further under the camper and pushed my hand into the gap. Yes, it was wide enough for a small kitten to crawl into. What's more, it felt very cool up there. We had filled up with water before leaving Evia that morning, and it had remained relatively cool in spite of the furnace-like conditions of the day. The clever little kitten had sussed this out and exploited the cooler location to the max, much to the chagrin of his worried guardians.

The following morning, we were up and away early to continue our journey to Krioneri along the north coast of the Gulf of Corinth. It's a quiet, picturesque route with beautiful views across the sea. Beyond the historical fortress town of Nafpaktos, the Gulf of Corinth narrows at the Strait of Rion and then widens into the Gulf of Patras. Just a few miles past Nafpaktos, the Rio-Antirrio bridge connects mainland Greece to Patras and the Peloponnese. Officially called the Charilaos Trikoup

Bridge, it's one of the longest multi-span cable-stayed bridges in the world. But we weren't taking the bridge that day. We had another 20 miles to reach our destination: the beautiful little settlement and port of Krioneri.

From the main road to Messolonghi, just before the Evinos River bridge, there's a left turn in the road. Blink, and you'd miss this junction. In 2014, the first year we ever visited Krioneri, we fortunately didn't blink and ventured down that road, which brought us to this picturesque fishing port. There's a wide crescent-shaped bay with a pebbly beach and ample parking. However, the most striking feature of this place is the gigantic rock named Varasova. It creates a surreal backdrop to the tiny port at its base. This limestone mountain rises almost vertically to over 3,000 feet (917 metres).

According to local mythology, the Titans attempted to hurl the rock into the sea to bridge the gap between the two coasts. But the rock proved too heavy, even for Titans, and it fell where it lies today.

But the most spectacular feature of Varasova occurs only for a few fleeting moments every evening when the sun sets. At sunset, Varasova undergoes an amazing colour transformation, changing from grey/white to beige and then deep red. It's so stunning and never ceases to impress. I'll never forget the first time I visited here and how I immediately fell in love with Krioneri.

It was back in September 2014 when we stayed on the pebbly beach for several weeks, jumping in and out of the crystal clear waters like a pair of flying fish. Towards the end of September, it was Claire's birthday, and to celebrate, we walked around the port to find a restaurant.

As it was already late in the season, most of the beach bars and dining venues were shut. However, straight ahead of us was a fish restaurant. It was around 6:00 p.m., and the place appeared deserted. Most Greeks don't dine until much later in the evening, so we weren't sure if it was for this reason there were no other customers or if it was also shut for the season.

We ventured inside the patio-style dining area and glanced around, looking for a sign of life. Just as we decided to abandon the idea of a birthday celebration, a figure emerged from the shadows of the kitchen area. The man approached us with his arms outstretched in a welcoming gesture and a smile that could brighten the darkest corners of a room. He introduced himself to us as Christos and welcomed us to his restaurant. Little did we realise that this random encounter would be the beginning of a wonderful and enduring friendship with Christos and his whole family.

Christos ushered us to a table with a beautiful view across the bay. Then I spotted the name *Captain del Mare* next to the entrance. Like so many in Greece, *Captain del Mare* is a family-run affair, and we quickly learned that it wasn't just a meal out—it was a dining experience.

Christos took our order and quickly disappeared into the kitchen, reemerging almost instantly with a basket of sliced bread, our shared Greek salad, a bottle of water, a pitcher of wine, a plate of marinated sardelles and a portion of Greek fava. The latter was a highly recommended addition and something we had never tasted before. A simple but delicious dip made from yellow split peas, it certainly did compliment the marinated sardines much to the beaming satisfaction of Christos, who had made the suggestion.

As there were no other customers to occupy his time, he joined us for a glass of wine after we'd finished our main course. In conversation, I mentioned that our meal was actually to celebrate Claire's birthday. The mere mention of the word birthday prompted another rapid disappearing act by Christos into the kitchen. Moments later, he reappeared, with his infectious laughter, clutching two slices of cake. The slice he handed to Claire had a sparkling candle flickering on top. *"Chrónia Pollá!......*Happy Birthday!" he cried out, followed by more laughter.

From that moment on, we fully realised that we were in the presence of a host with the most charismatic, generous, friendly, humourous, affectionate, good-hearted character. And that was just our first encounter with the one and only Christos Paganias.

From the National road to Messolonghi, we made that left turn and continued on to the end. Another sharp turn, and we had arrived. Just like every other year, it seemed like we were returning home, that all the time that had passed in between had evaporated into thin air.

Also, this visit was extra special because we had missed out in the previous year due to the worldwide COVID restrictions.

We parked just opposite *Captain del Mare* and raced over to greet our Greek family. Christos was the first one we met, followed by his brother and top chef, Giórgos, their sister Giorgina, Giórgos's wife Stella, their kids Magda, Maria, and little Yianni, and grandma Maria.

It felt so great to be back in their company and share lots of hugs, greetings, and laughter. As it was now mid-morning, we went back to the camper and let the family prepare for another busy lunchtime at *The Captain.*

Only a short drive around the small crescent bay we found our grassy spot just next to the pebbly beach. The same spot we'd been parking on since 2014. Vangelis was the first to exit through the camper's side habitation door.

He had been patiently waiting for us while we had been catching up with Christos and his family. He stretched forward, yawned and proceeded to sniff out his new surroundings. Then he wandered down to the water's edge for further sniffing.

One minor worry about this particular beach was the number of stray dogs around. Over the years we'd become acquainted with some of them and had even given them names. They were just big, unfortunate, unwanted animals with one thing in common: hunger.

They'd become accustomed to scavenging a few scraps from the occasional visitors in camper vans. In other words, they'd associated large white vehicles with a possible free lunch. So it was a nagging worry that one, or more, might see Vangelis and attack him. But our worries proved to be futile.

Two big, hungry hounds came ambling along the dusty beach road that afternoon. When they spotted our camper, they just ambled on over, their tongues dangling and dripping as they panted in the heat. Vangelis was underneath, behind the back wheel, sheltering in the shade. I watched carefully as they approached within two metres from the camper when suddenly Vangelis shot out, bouncing sideways, all bushed up. He was spitting and snarling furiously at them.

The dogs stopped and stared at him, stunned, as if they had been thunderstruck. Then they looked at each other before proceeding along the dusty road, foregoing any opportunity for a free bite to eat. Vangelis continued to monitor their departure before withdrawing to the shade once more. *"Wow, that kitten can certainly pack a punch,"* I thought to myself. *"Nothing to worry about there."*

That same day, we had another surprise when Claire received a private message on her Instagram page. It was from a website called Love Meow (LoveMeow.com), a cat lovers' site dedicated to publishing the latest news and original stories on cats, kittens and cat rescue.

The sender wrote:

Thank you for rescuing Vangelis! He is absolutely adorable I'm a writer from Love Meow, a cat news site. We are interested in doing a story on the kitten and spreading the cute! Could you tell us a bit about how he came to you? Was he a stray/shy/friendly/cuddly? When was the moment you knew he had chosen you? How would you describe his personality? What are some of his favourite things to do? Thank you so much for giving him a home! The world needs more people like you!

Claire, of course, responded immediately with all the details and also provided photos. Just days later, the article was featured on the Love Meow website and appeared on their Facebook page with the headline:

"Kitten comes bounding up to a couple on a beach and asks to travel with them."

Following this remarkable incident, Claire searched online to see if other websites had picked up on the story. Sure enough, she found a full-featured article in La Stampa, the oldest newspaper in Italy based in Turin.

The headline read:

"Coppia in vacanza in Grecia incontra un gatto randagio: Così Vangelis ci ha scelti come sua nuova famiglia"

(Couple on holiday in Greece encounters a stray cat: This is how Vangelis chose us as his new family.)

That Italian story also featured a very cute photo of Vangelis sitting on one of our outdoor chairs. But there was more.

A few days after arriving in Krioneri, a French motorhome pulled up a short distance from us. A nosy Vangelis, of course, had to wander over to check out the new arrivals. I could see he was making waves with the couple's little daughter. It didn't seem like he was making a nuisance of himself, but I decided to approach them and at least introduce him.

As I chatted with the little girl's Dad, I recounted the story of the kitten playing enthusiastically with his daughter next to us. We were speaking in French, and as I elaborated on the kitten's tale, his eyes widened, and his expression turned almost to disbelief. *"Et vous? Vous êtes de L'île de Man?"* he asked me. I confirmed that yes, indeed, I was from the Isle of Man. He then cried out to his wife inside the camper. *"Marceline! C'est lui. C'est le chaton de l'île d'Eubée. Incroyable!"* which translated means: *"Marceline! It's him. The kitten from Evia. Unbelievable!"*

He excitedly told me that they were animal lovers and that the Vangelis story had been featured in a French animal welfare website they followed. He started snapping photos of the lively kitten now spinning in circles after a feather the little girl was taunting him with.

Once the Vangelis Show Time was over, I wished the family a *"bonne soirée"* and walked back to the camper with the celebrity kitten writhing in my arms. The Frenchman had said, *"Unbelievable,"* which certainly seemed the most appropriate word. Within only two weeks and a few days, the story had gone viral worldwide. But there was even more!

The day after encountering the French family, we drove the short distance to Messolonghi, Greece's Holy City. We always park just outside the main shopping and pedestrian area, next to the Garden of Heroes, within the city walls. That morning, just as we had parked up and were on foot to the centre, a cyclist shot past, waving his hand in the air and crying out, *"Isle of Man! Isle of Man! Where is Vangelis?"*

It was just another extraordinary moment when a complete stranger crossed our path because of the abandoned kitten story. He stopped and introduced himself as *Staikos from Athens*. He was originally from Messolonghi and had picked up the story online, perhaps because of a mutual connection to Krioneri.

Anyway, cycling past the parked camper, he noticed the Isle of Man registration number and quickly deduced it must be Vangelis's van. He stopped, dismounted, and asked to meet the famous kitten. After introductions and some light-hearted chit-chat, we agreed we should meet again soon for coffee. *The Messenger of Good News* was proving, again and again, to be a very appropriate aptronym for the miracle kitty.

There is a proud and noble reason why Messolonghi is referred to as Greece's Holy City. It earned this title due to the heroic defence of the inhabitants in 1826 against the Turks who had besieged the city for one year.

An armed exit failed after a traitor leaked the plan to the Turks. An estimated three thousand Greek men were killed during the Exodus of Messolonghi. Six thousand women and children were taken as slaves and sold to the slave markets of Constantinople and Alexandria.

It is widely accepted that the sacrifices at Messolonghi led to international support for the Greek cause and would prove decisive in helping the Greeks win the war and gain their independence. The fate of those incredibly brave citizens of the city is honoured every year with magnificent parades and ceremonies with participants from all over the country.

Back on the beach at Krioneri, we noticed that the French camper had departed, but another one had arrived. It was parked much further along from us in the shade of several trees. It was too far away for a busybody kitten to trek to, so I wasn't concerned he would intrude on the new arrivals.

On the subject of the busybody kitten, we still hadn't decided what to do about him. We knew a local woman who had sheltered many stray dogs, but she showed no interest in little Vangelis when we asked her. Yana's prediction that it would be difficult, in Greece, to find a loving forever home for him was proving accurate.

That evening, after dinner, we stayed up long after dark playing backgammon under a star-filled night sky. Vangelis played nearby, occasionally pouncing on our feet and nipping our ankles, forever the attention seeker.

Just before bedtime, we heard the trudge-trudge of feet on the pebbles approaching from the direction of Krioneri. As the sound got louder, we saw the silhouette of a couple close to the water's edge. As they passed in front, they wished us a *"Guten Abend."* It was the couple from the camper parked further along the beach. So I replied with a *"Danke, gleichfalls guten Abend,"* as they continued on their way. It was now bedtime, so we packed away our backgammon game, arranged the table and chairs and decided to head inside. *"Where's Vangelis?"* asked Claire. *"Oh, he's just….here….."* But he wasn't.

"He was just here, only seconds ago." I replied anxiously. I crouched down to look under the camper while Claire grabbed a torch and a bag of kitten treats. Back outside, we began a thorough search of the immediate area, shaking the bag of his favourite treats and calling out his name. I paid particular attention to his cool corner above the fresh water tank under the camper. But there was no sign of him anywhere.

We widened the search, both going opposite directions, before circling back. Our anxiety now turned to a nagging worry. After an hour of searching and calling out his name, we decided we should get some sleep and continue the search at daybreak. We left the camper's side door wide open and his food dish on the step.

It was a very restless night indeed. The slightest noise from outside woke us both, and we bolted upright, checking to see if our little comrade had come home. But there was nothing.

I kept the door open all night but brought his food dish in from the step just in case it would attract any stray dogs. I must have fallen asleep at some point because, around 05:00, I woke up, and for a split second, my waking brain was oblivious to the previous night's events.

But then the reality of the moment painfully kicked in, and anguish swept over me, realising that Vangelis had now been missing for over seven hours.

It was still dark outside, so I made coffee while we formulated a search and rescue plan. Most of the land beyond the beach is for agricultural purposes and is divided into large blocks of up to ten acres apiece. Access roads for tractors and farm equipment run adjacent to the fields.

We decided to split up and walk the length and breadth of each block of land, calling out his name and rattling bags of cat treats. Meeting up halfway around, we'd move on to the next block of land. We covered a large area, often going back on ourselves, checking the drainage ditches and long grass that ran next to the single-track roads. But there was no sign of him anywhere. It was now approaching mid-morning and the sun was already blazing down on us. This only added to our worries as we knew he'd be very thirsty by now, wherever he was.

When we met up, after another broad sweep of the area, I suggested going even further to cover the next block of land. Even though we both knew it was unlikely he'd wander that far away, it was worth a try. Anything was worth a try. We stayed together and walked along the narrow road with wide fields on either side of us. In the distance, I saw a shepherd with his flock. I also saw three big sheepdogs prowling around the perimeter of the grazing sheep, and I had to quickly bury the negative thoughts I was having.

We reached a four-way junction, turned left, and walked 300 metres back to the beach. From this point, turning left again, it was a distance of about 500 metres back to the camper. As we trudged along the hot, dusty road, I could see the copse of trees ahead of us on the right beside the seashore, where the other camper had parked the day before. As we approached, I noticed it had a German registration number. My brain started to engage and process this incoming information: a German camper and a *"Guten Abend"* last night from a German couple passing by; seconds later, Vangelis is missing.

"There he is!" shrieked Claire. And sure enough, over by one of the trees, was a very unhappy and distressed-looking kitten. Claire cried out his name, and he came bounding over to her immediately. She picked him up for a huge cuddle, and from where I was standing, all I could hear was loud purring.

My brain went into overdrive processing the latest incoming information. *"He must have followed the Germans to their camper last night,"* I exclaimed.

It was the only explanation. During the brief seconds after the German couple passed by, we were getting ready to go inside, and Vangelis must have skipped off after them. At some point, he must have become disorientated and followed the couple to their camper. He must have spent the entire night there, possibly confusing their camper for ours. Once we got him back, he tucked into his favourite kitty biscuits and gulped down half a bowl of water. Then, he slept for the rest of the morning.

Later that afternoon, my speculation on our furry Houdini's latest disappearing act was confirmed. We were sitting outside, under the shade, with Vangelis by our side when a middle-aged couple approached from the direction of the German camper. As they approached, the woman exclaimed, *"Ah, schau mal, das ist das Kätzchen von gestern Abend." ("Look, it's the kitten from last night.")*

They then asked if he was our kitten and proceeded to explain that the previous evening, just as they reached their camper, he was there at their feet. *"He wanted to enter our camper and was very determined too"* she continued, *"but we didn't want him inside."*

I was feeling a bit annoyed because of all the stress and worry this had caused us, but I said nothing. Then she remarked, *"It's not normal for a kitten to appear on a beach from nowhere, is it?"* Of course, I couldn't disagree with her on that assumption.

We stayed another few days in Krioneri before making a snap decision to return to Evia. My friend Nick, in Athens, had been in touch to let us know he was due a few days off work and wanted to meet up somewhere. It would have been a six hour round trip for him to come to Krioneri, so we compromised and decided on Evia for lunch. The following morning, I went to *Captain del Mare* to tell Christos we'd be away for a week or so but fully intended on coming back to Krioneri. It was still early in the day, and he had time for a chat. Over coffee, he told me a remarkable story about his father and grandfather, particularly his grandfather's small fishing boat.

During the Second World War, under the German occupation, travel anywhere was very restricted, both on land and sea. Christos's grandfather had been on a clandestine trip with his 10-year-old son (Christos's dad) on their small boat. The purpose of the journey was to bring provisions into Krioneri port.

Just as he had docked and started offloading, a German Luftwaffe aircraft appeared overhead. The activity below caught the pilot's eye, and he responded with a low pass, shooting up the fishing boat and another moored next to it. No one was injured, but both vessels were destroyed and sank.

In 2000, Krioneri saw the construction of a new harbour built alongside the existing one to shelter visiting yachts. During the work, the wreckage of both sunken boats was discovered, and parts of the remains were hauled up to the surface. Under the wreckage of the boat that belonged to Christos's grandfather, a case of wine was discovered intact. Christos explained to the workers that the boat where the wine was found belonged to his grandfather, and the wine, therefore, belonged to him! But, in Christos's own words, *"Of course, I didn't keep it for myself! We opened the bottles and drank the wine all together, and it was wonderful!"*

Just opposite *Captain del Mare*, there is an old single railway line. It runs past Christos's restaurant and ends abruptly at the old port. Further along the road, towards the pebbly beach where we park, there are also the remains of an antiquated railway station, now almost obscured by trees. From here, this rusting railway track continues towards the village of Galatas before veering west in the direction of Messolonghi.

"Oh, it's just an old railway station," I was told some years ago when I asked about the dilapidated building barely visible from the road. It turned out to be a rather

143

dismissive comment for something once part of a wonderful service for many thousands of people.

Arriving at the small port of Krioneri, a visitor might notice the single-track railway line—or maybe not. These days, it's almost buried in the asphalt laid in 1990. From the harbour, this long, disused single track disappears into the long grass and a wooded area, almost disappearing without a trace. I was always curious about its history, and it was only in more recent times, and with Christos's local knowledge, that I discovered just how important this railway had been throughout its over eighty years of service.

The first motor car to ever appear in Greece was in Athens in 1897. The city's citizens were astonished and amazed by the sight of this "self-propelled vehicle," as horse-drawn carriages were still the only known mode of transport. However, that car was soon returned to its manufacturers in Germany because it was useless in Athens.

A writer at the time wrote: *How could it be possible to drive a machine of such fine composition on roads that were not only unsuitable but also dangerous?*

If the state of roads in Athens was so bad in 1897, imagine how poor the conditions were elsewhere in the country at that time. Nevertheless, 10 years earlier, the Prime Minister, Charilaos Trikoupis, signed a contract that would fulfil his ingenious and inventive vision.

A railway linking Agrinio, Western Greece's second largest city, to the port of Patras in the Peloponnese. The railway would connect Agrino to Messolonghi, a distance of about 36 miles, and then continue to Krioneri, where a ferry service would cross the narrow sea passage to Patras.

The train service was for both commercial and passenger purposes. Local seasonal products were shipped south by rail and, from the port of Patras, could reach the rest of Greece and also be exported to other countries. The main network was completed within two years, followed by the extension to Krioneri.

In fact, by 1891, the Krioneri—Agrinio railway line operated with a steam train, with stations starting at the port of Krioneri and including Galatas, Evinochori, Messolonghi, Alykes, Aitoliko, Stamna, Angelokastro, Dokimi, and, finally, Agrinio. The whole journey took two hours and thirty five minutes, and the average speed was 15 mph (24 km/hour).

Krioneri became the connecting hub for this wonderful train service. The harbour and ferryboat were specially adapted to accommodate the goods wagons, which were transported directly onto the ferry to save offloading and loading times. A single locomotive with up to ten wagons could be loaded at any one time. The rail link, of course, brought great prosperity to the port settlement.

Farmers, producers and small manufacturers all benefitted from the service. It opened up a whole new world of transportation and connection for thousands of citizens who could now travel and visit friends and family across the region. Local business flourished as merchants and farmers traded their goods of rice, beans, lentils, maize, salt, and tobacco. Of course, back then, the Rio-Antirrio suspension bridge didn't exist, and there was no main road beyond Krioneri.

Sadly, this fantastic service came to a halt in February 1970 when the line was disbanded. Thus, an era of train travel that had served the country so well for over eighty years ended.

These days, a four-lane motorway, along with the main national road, connects the towns and cities. Most of Greece's motorway network was completed in 2017 at a cost of over 13 billion euros. The motorway tolls are amongst the highest in Europe, and the overall construction costs have only added to the country's already burgeoning debt.

I once made my way through the undergrowth and trees to see the old railway station up close. I spent a whole morning taking photos and trying to imagine how it must have been back in its heyday.

What was once an elegant building thoughtfully designed and constructed is now in ruins. The roof is collapsing, and the interior has fallen to pieces. What would have been a waiting room with toilet facilities, a ticket office, and perhaps a small refreshments area are long gone.

In front of the station, the railway lines are still lying on their sleepers with a set of points at either end. I could almost imagine the sounds of steam trains arriving and departing, their whistles blowing, and the sight of the station master with passengers disembarking along with excited children on their first train trip to the seaside. The whole experience would have amounted to more than just a rail service; for many, it would have been a social event!

It is a crying shame that such a beneficial and wonderful resource should be discarded, disposed of, and abandoned after many years of faithful service. Could parts of the railway line not have been preserved if only for tourism? Could the old station not have been retained as a café or restaurant? Better still, could it not have been kept as a small museum to honour the legacy of what was surely once a very valuable service to all who used and benefitted from it?

Christos's father was one of the very first residents of Krioneri after the war. He came from a nearby village called Káto Vasilikí, located on the other side of the giant rock Varasova.

In the beginning, he had a herd of sheep and a few horses, but later, he rented a shop on the old port of Krioneri where he sold souvlakis and soft drinks to the passing train passengers. Back in those times, there was no mains electricity, and he had an obligation to run a generator to provide light in the port during the disembarkation and boarding of passengers from the train service.

When the ship left, the generator shut down, and again, the small village was in the dark. Sadly, I never had the opportunity to meet Christos's father, but by all accounts, he was a very popular, well-loved, larger-than-life character with infectious laughter. Christos has certainly inherited many of his father's characteristics, particularly his laughter. If you ever visit *Captain del Mare*, Krioneri, you will hear him before you see him!

****

Chapter Six

Return to Evia

After my early morning chat and coffee with Christos, I returned to the camper, and we got ready to leave for Evia. We said goodbye to our friends in Krioneri and promised to return in a week or so, then headed to the main road towards Nafpaktos.

There was another reason I wanted to return to Evia: my dentist's mum! In the Isle of Man, my dentist, Thanos, is Greek. During a dental checkup back in December 2019, I expressed a yearning to improve my Greek to him. As he was staring down at my mouth, inspecting my teeth with a mask on and bright dental lights blinding me, he suggested that I should seek help online. Maybe a teacher or a Greek speaker willing to help with vocabulary.

I agreed with him and replied that this was indeed a great idea, and all I had to do was find such a person. But I don't think he understood a word I said, as a dental aspirator was siphoning the back of my oral cavity while he was evaluating my gums and teeth with a periodontal probe.

After my checkup, I paid the bill at reception and headed for the door. Suddenly, Thanos appeared from his surgery and exclaimed, *"My mum is a teacher. She has never done online teaching, but if it's just to help you speak the language better, maybe she can help."*

And that's how it started. I'd connect via Facetime twice a month with Thanos's mum, Dina, who lives in Chalkida, the capital of Evia. She would send me a long text to translate, and I would write a short story or anecdote in Greek. The lessons lasted around an hour, which certainly got me out of a rut with the language. Also, as the winter of 2020 progressed into the COVID-19 spring and the lockdown blues, these lessons proved invaluable for maintaining sound, balanced mental health for both of us.

As we were a little late leaving Krioneri, we broke up the return journey to Evia, once again, at Anemokámpi beach near Galaxidi. It was another hot afternoon, and as soon as we stopped, Vangelis leapt out of the camper and headed underneath. Only this time, we knew where he was. I got down on my stomach and slithered below the chassis, and just above the fresh water tank, I could see two beady eyes staring back down at me.

He stayed there for the rest of the afternoon, reappearing only for a bite to eat and a drink of water. It was so hot outside that I wished I could have crawled up and joined him next to the cool water tank.

The following day, we stayed at the beach until midafternoon as we were in no hurry to reach Evia. The arrangement to meet up with Dina was for the late afternoon; from Galaxidi, it's only about a three hour drive.

Any city centre in Greece in the middle of summer will be hot and stifling, especially for a little kitten. Dina had provided us with details of a large parking lot near her apartment and close to a small bay. When we got there, we parked in the shade of some trees facing the small bay, where a cool sea breeze was blowing. We then sent a text message, and my Greek tutor arrived 15 minutes later. It was lovely to finally meet up in person, and after introducing Dina to both Claire and Vangelis, we walked to her apartment to meet her partner, Nickos and enjoyed a few cold drinks out on the balcony.

Nicko's daughter Melina arrived shortly after, and we all headed out for dinner. I insisted on stopping by the camper to make sure Vangelis was alright. When Melina spotted him, it was love at first sight! She couldn't put him down, and I honestly believe she would have happily foregone dinner just to sit and pamper him for an hour or two longer. Claire looked at me, and I knew instantly what she was thinking. Was Melina going to be Vangelis's forever home?

We strolled along a wide public promenade next to the Evripos channel, leading to the old historic Evripos bridge. We were in the downtown area of Chalkida, and it was absolutely buzzing with life. This long thoroughfare is lined with many cafés, restaurants, and bars and it certainly has a very exciting cosmopolitan feel.

We all settled on classic Greek gyros with a few beers for dinner at one of Dina and Niko's favourite bar and grill restaurants. It was a lovely evening and a lot of fun catching up, finally, with my online Greek tutor.

We talked endlessly about Vangelis and how his story had reached so many people worldwide. Melina was clearly enamoured but, by the end of the evening, it was obvious that she couldn't adopt him as she was in her last year at university. It wouldn't be practical to have the added responsibility of a boisterous kitten in her student accommodation. At the end of the evening, we all headed back to the camper and said goodnight.

Vangelis got one last cuddle from Melina, and then we drove the short distance from Chalkida back to the beach Paraliakí Poseidónos near Lefkandi. It was pitch dark when we arrived, and after parking next to the tree-lined beach, we all three of us settled in and fell fast asleep.

Nick and Helen arrived from Loutsa the following morning around 11:00. The last time we'd seen them was in February 2020, when we'd flown to Athens for a quick winter break. Luckily, we made it home just weeks before the wider world began shutting down and locking down.

But, like all solid friendships, the passage of time made no difference when we met up. You pick up where you left off, and 18 months feels like sometime last week.

Vangelis was loitering in the long grass and shrubbery next to a tree and immediately made his presence known to our guests. Moments after we were all seated outside the camper, he pounced on Helen's ankles. She was quick to thwart his assault and declared, *"So this is the little rascal who has cancelled your visit to see us at home?"*

Their dog, Molly, is large and lively and gets very excited around everyone and everything. It didn't seem plausible that this small kitten, now gnawing at Nick's ankles, could pose a threat to the big, bouncy Molly. But when I detailed the encounter with stray dogs on Krioneri beach and how the diminutive Vangelis can pack a powerful punch, they quickly understood. A visit to Loutsa would have meant separating them, and that would have involved keeping Vangelis locked inside the camper in the blistering heat. That was not an option we would have dared consider.

After a few swims, more coffees and endless chatter, we all decided to head to Lefkandi for lunch. The small seaside town was very busy, but we still found a very nice taverna close to the beach, with plenty of shade and a gentle sea breeze.

The afternoon seemed to fly by, and it wasn't long before we had the usual concerns for Vangelis. He was back inside the camper with the roof windows wide open, a fan whirring at full speed, and several cold bottles of water strategically placed around his bed to keep him cooled down. *"You're like two worried parents on the first day of nursery school,"* joked Helen. And it was true. It was now over three weeks since this rollercoaster ride had begun, and it seemed like everything we did or planned to do revolved around this celebrity kitten.

We were still no further on in deciding what to do about him either. We had a ferry booked for October 12th from Greece back to Italy, followed by a 1,400-mile drive to the Isle of Man. And all that was only about eight weeks away.

Nick also added some food for thought. He's one of those pensive, reflective thinks-things-through types, so his input and advice are often well-balanced, rational, and compos mentis. *"If you do decide to keep him, be sure and check out all the requirements before returning to the UK,"* he said. This was followed by *"because it's possible that many vets, here in Greece, might not be that familiar with the UK regulations."*

His words were like a brush with authority. Rules and regulations, laws and formalities. How easy it is to forget about our regulated and controlled world when you're enjoying a nomadic lifestyle in a camper van.

Anyway, Nick's recommendations were duly noted and understood. We returned to the camper to find Vangelis comfortably curled up and fast asleep on the driver's seat. Our earlier concerns proved to be wholly unnecessary as he woke up, stared over, and opened his mouth to its full width to let out a big yawn.

Helen and Nick had to get back to Loutsa shortly after, so we said our goodbyes and hoped the next get-together wouldn't be another 18 months away.

The following morning, I was up very early, as usual, to let Vangelis out. The early morning light was breaking, and down by the shoreline, I could make out the silhouettes of the sea anglers. Vangelis had spotted them, too, because he was already halfway across the sand, making his way to his beach buddies. At least he was wandering off to the *safe side* of the beach. Even during these early hours, there were occasionally fast-moving cars, vans and mopeds on the road behind us.

As I went about my morning duties of setting up the table and chairs, rolling out the awning, and topping up the fresh water tank, I could hear several voices and laughter from the shoreline as the fishermen greeted their returning buddy. It really amused me to hear several of them refer to him by his name. *"Yeia sou Vangelis!"* Clearly, this curious kitten had left a lasting impression on them the first time around. Once again, their fishing lures, floats, bait, and accessories would keep him entertained for at least enough time for us to enjoy a morning cup of coffee in peace.

Around 10:00 that same morning, a familiar old white Suzuki jeep parked not far from us. It was Yana with her two small dogs in tow. As she set up her lounge bed in the shade of the trees, she smiled and waved over.

"Kalós írthete," I heard her say as she welcomed us back. Shortly after, I went over it for a chat. I told her

about our short trip to Krioneri, meeting up with friends in Chalkida and Nick and Helen's visit the day before.

That morning, Yana's kind, caring, and affectionate demeanour appeared to mask a despondency and melancholy. There was sadness in her eyes when, unexpectedly, she started to speak about her late husband.

She looked straight ahead, out to sea, as she recounted how she had lost him precisely one year earlier. From the first diagnosis until he died, the cancer had taken her man from her in only a matter of weeks.

"He was fit and well one day and then gone the next," she continued. I didn't say a word; I just let her speak as I believed that was all she wanted to do. To give her grief and sorrow a voice.

She spoke at length about her difficulties with paperwork and state bureaucracy because her husband had left no final instructions, disposition, will, or testimony. And then, in an instant, she ended her heartbroken reminiscence, wiped away a tear, turned and smiled, and asked, *"What about your little kitten Vangelis, what's happening with him?"*

I told her how he was currently entertaining the guys, fishing by the water's edge, and that his future was still somewhat uncertain. I proceeded to say that we hadn't quite managed to find a home for him yet and that it was proving difficult to do so when she interrupted me with a raised hand. I stopped talking as she gently spoke the following words:

"Animals have a purpose when they come into our lives, so keep Vangelis and take him home with you."

It was like an assertion or endorsement that I had unconsciously been waiting for. Yana wasn't telling us what to do. She was simply confirming what we wanted to hear. Right then and there, I knew there would be no further questions or doubts. Vangelis was coming home with us. All we had to do was figure out the procedures and formulate an action plan. I couldn't wait to tell Claire! I wished Yana a lovely day and raced back over to the camper.

"Guess what?" I said. But before I could complete my grand announcement, Claire pointed at the floor mat and said, *"Please, can you do something about that first?"* A small dead fish covered in sand and dirt was lying on the mat. *"The guys fishing must have given it to Vangelis, and he has gifted it to us,"* she said, with a roll of the eyes.

I picked the small sprat up by the tail and looked left and right before discarding it into the long grass next to the trees. *"What was it you wanted to say, love?"* she asked.

I stopped sniffing the fishy odour on the finger and thumb of my right hand, looked up, smiled and announced: *"Vangelis, he's coming home with us. No ifs or buts, it's settled!"* Claire looked absolutely delighted and said, *"I'm not iffing or butting at all, but what brought this on?"* I told her about my conversation with Yana and how she had spoken in depth about the loss of her husband before offering up her own words of wisdom regarding Vangelis.

We were both so glad that a decision had been made. The truth is that we had unnecessarily dithered for too long about what to do. Since the moment Vangelis had arrived at our camper on the beach in Evia we had been hesitant about travelling with a pet. But here we were, nearly four weeks later, doing exactly that! And apart from a couple of disappearing acts and high anxiety moments, we'd loved every moment of it. And so had thousands of Vangelis followers online.

It was close to the weekend, so we decided to wait until the following Sunday before returning to Messolonghi. We knew a vet in the town from a previous trip when we'd helped a Dutch guy get help for his poorly dog. It made sense to get Vangelis's health checkup, vaccinations, and passport all sorted out in Messolonghi. If there were any delays, we could always wait them out just around the corner in Krioneri.

So, the following Sunday morning, we packed up again for the drive back to Western Greece. There was just one last thing I needed to do before leaving Evia, and that was to say goodbye to our friend Yana.

Sure enough, around 10:00 am, a familiar white Suzuki jeep appeared and parked nearby. We went over to tell Yana about our travel plans and thank her for her kindness and all the gifts she'd brought for Vangelis and ourselves. I also thanked her for the advice she'd given me. She looked a little confused at this, so I repeated her words from a few days earlier:

"Animals have a purpose when they come into our lives."
And, with that, we said goodbye.

****

Our trip back to Western Greece was broken up with another overnight stop at Galaxidi and, from there, we reached Messolonghi early on the Monday morning. The red plastic pet carrier box Yana had given us would now be put to full use. I had managed to secure the damaged door hinge with a couple of cable ties and Claire had crocheted a small blanket for the inside.

After finding a place to park the camper, we opened the pet carrier, set it on the floor, and waited to see what Vangelis would do. He went straight in, on his own, without any hesitation. His inquisitive nature had got the better of him, and the sight of the open box was too much to resist. We secured the door to the carrier, locked up the camper, and headed into town.

The vet's surgery was about a 15-minute walk away, but Vangelis never complained once. There wasn't as much as a peep out of him. He just sat inside, his face almost pressed against the plastic grill door, taking in all the sights and sounds and the hustle and bustle of an early morning Greek town.

There were two other customers ahead of us at the vet's. Both had large dogs with them; still, Vangelis never murmured once. When it was our turn, the vet appeared flustered and distracted. Just as I went to speak, he answered an incoming call on his phone while trying to placate another customer who had just arrived, barging his way to the front of the queue with questions about his dog's ear infection. Meanwhile, a woman wanted to pay for some cat food whilst complaining about the other customer for muscling his way in front of her. It was like shopping at Lidl on a bad day.

Finally, the vet turned to me, and I managed to explain to him, in as few words as possible, that we had a kitten in the box and needed a pet passport. I had already learned and rehearsed many keywords like *"diavatírio, emvólio* and *lýssa"* (*passport, vaccination and rabies*) just in case of a language problem. Anyway, he just replied, *"Let's have a look at him,"* took the box from me and went through to his surgery with both of us following closely behind.

Vangelis behaved very well when he checked his heart rate, ears, mouth, and eyes. It was only when his body temperature was checked, using a thermometer inserted into the opposite end of his body, that he protested. He lashed out at the offending hand holding the thermometer with one of his big paws.

The vet still hadn't answered my enquiry about a pet passport, so I asked again if he could provide this service. He seemed irritated by my question and replied, *"Of course I can! But the passport will need to be ordered from Athens. We don't keep them in stock. It will take about three to four days to arrive."*

He then completed the health check and estimated that Vangelis was about eight weeks old. *"I can give him a flu vaccination and micro-chip him today, but you'll have to bring him back in a week for the rabies vaccination,"* he said. At eight weeks old, he was still too young for the rabies jab, and receiving two vaccinations on the same day wasn't recommended anyway. Apparently, at nine weeks, most kittens are fully weaned, and the antibodies they've got from their mother's milk are no longer active in their systems. Vangelis obviously had zero antibodies from his mother's milk, as he'd been with us since he was four weeks old.

A large syringe-like instrument was placed against his left shoulder, and a microchip was inserted. This was followed by his flu jab. The vet gave us the empty flu vaccination vial along with a barcode sticker accompanying the microchip. *"Don't lose these things because the information on them must be entered into the passport."* With that, we were ushered back into the waiting room as the vet shouted out, *"Next, please,"* to a packed house. I wanted to tell him, *"Please don't forget to order the passport,"* but I decided against it because he looked completely exasperated by his day so far. We assumed payment would be settled later once the whole procedure was completed.

As we strolled back to the camper, Claire commented on the vet's attitude and apparent lack of enthusiasm. *"What did you think of him?"* she asked. I shrugged my shoulders and said, *"Maybe he's just having a bad day."* *"But it's only 10:00 in the morning,"* Claire replied.

We spent the week in Krioneri, enjoying loads of fun afternoons by the beach with Stella and her kids. Then, the following Monday, we went back to Messolonghi to finalise the pet passport and the rabies jab. It was now August 30th, and we had exactly six weeks remaining before our ferry departure from Greece to Italy. The vet's surgery was packed with customers and an array of pets, all requiring some sort of attention. It was taking so long that Claire decided to save time and leave me with Vangelis to complete other errands she had. *"Just text me when you're done, and I'll meet you back here."*

When it was finally Vangelis's turn, I approached the vet, half expecting some kind of acknowledgement from him. It had been, after all, only a week since our previous visit. As soon as I reintroduced him to Vangelis and inquired about the passport, I knew instantly that he had forgotten to order it.

His eyes flicked from left to right, accompanied by an insincere smile, a sure sign of incoming baloney. *"Ah, it's been delayed. I have no idea why. I'll speak to them again,"* came the flood of excuses. *"But we can give Vangelis his rabies vaccination,"* he declared with a feigned smile. Once the jab had been administered, I urged him to order the passport as soon as possible, reminding him that we had to leave the area very soon. He nodded his head somewhat ruefully, which almost confirmed his forgetfulness.

Back in the waiting room, I saw Claire, who had just returned from her errands. *"How did it go?"* she asked. *"I'll tell you outside,"* came my reply. We were both a bit wary now of how this matter was progressing. We wanted to visit a few places in the Peloponnese before heading north to Prespas, but we couldn't plan anything until the pet passport arrived. So we returned to Krioneri to wait it out once again.

During the week, I called the vet's surgery to see if the elusive passport had arrived from Athens. I was told abruptly that it hadn't and to try again in a few days. We we made up our minds, then and there, that if there were any more delays, we'd be forced to go elsewhere.

The following Monday we decided to drive back over to Messologhi and show up at the vet's surgery in person instead of calling ahead of time. Outside the building, I noticed a small white van badly parked, half on the road and half on the pavement. The letters A.C.S. were written tall and proud on the side along with the slogan: *"Ta Pánta, Pantoú"* meaning *"Everything, Everywhere."* It was a Greek courier service, albeit one with a 93% one-star rating. The slogan *"Everything, Everywhere"* ought to be preceded by the words *"Sometimes we lose…."*

But maybe, just maybe, there was a pet passport amongst the small pile of packets that had just fallen from the back of the van onto the road as the driver opened the rear doors.

We entered the vet's, and thankfully, there was only one other customer ahead of us at the counter. The vet glanced over, probably recognised the red box containing Vangelis, and immediately turned his attention to a small pile of packets and envelopes that had just been deposited on the counter by the courier.

He continued his conversation with the customer while simultaneously fidgeting with the small pile of packets. He was clearly a master at multitasking because seconds after his customer turned to leave, he removed a blue EU pet passport from an envelope, waved it in the air, and announced, *"It has arrived!"*

We'd brought Vangelis with us just in case the vet wanted to see him again. As this wasn't necessary, Claire left me to sort out the details of the passport and returned to the camper with Vangelis.

Sitting at his computer, the vet asked me for my address in Greece. *"I don't have one; we're here as tourists,"* I replied. The next question was regarding a Greek A.F.M. number. This is a tax identification number all Greeks and residents must have in order to do practically anything in life within the country. Again, I had to explain that we were only visitors and not residents and, therefore, didn't have an A.F.M. He waved his hand dismissively, signalling that none of this mattered, but then asked for my passport number, which I could not provide right then and there. Again, this detail was brushed off as if it didn't matter anyway.

He then asked me to fill in my name and full address in the appropriate section of the passport. After I handed it back, he asked for the vaccine vials and the microchip barcode stickers. The vaccine labels from the vials were stuck into the passport. The vaccination date and the renewal date were entered in by hand. Same with the microchip barcode and number. Then, he asked about Vangelis's date of birth. I dutifully explained that he had first appeared on July 24th, and we had estimated his age at four weeks old. Counting backwards, his approximate date of birth would be June 26th, 2021. A few more mouse clicks and key taps followed on his computer before he signed off the passport's vaccination entries and handed the document over to me. The whole procedure cost 50 euros, not to mention one week's worth of suspense, nail-biting, and apprehension.

Outside in the street, under the warm September sunshine, I felt a renewed sense of calmness return. Acquiring Vangelis's passport felt like a small achievement, and with this administrative obstacle out of the way, we could enjoy our remaining weeks in Greece.

****

Peloponnese

We hadn't visited the Peloponnese since 2011, and the reason for this 10-year gap was simply because the summer months had become too busy across this southern Greek region. However, this was 2021, the second year of the COVID pandemic, and, as we'd already discovered, vast numbers of visitors had chosen to stay at home.

So, we set off across the middle of the Peloponnese peninsula towards Kalamata via Tripoli. Just west of Kalamata is Messini, where there is a fantastic beach called Bouka. It's over two miles long, and there wasn't another person in sight when we arrived. I could only imagine how busy this beautiful stretch of sand would ordinarily be in normal times.

We parked up on the beach's western end, close to a breakwater constructed from large rocks. We stayed several days there, and Vangelis spent most of his time exploring the gaps in the rocks along the breakwater.

He'd occasionally saunter back to the camper for a bite to eat and a snooze before returning to his rocky playground. If he was gone for too long, we'd have to take turns walking over the large rocks and boulders, calling out his name and waiting for the telltale chime of his collar bells. Even though he was growing fast, he was still a smallish kitten, and the crevices between some of the rocks were deep. On more than a few occasions, I'd have to lie flat on my stomach to reach into the gaps to haul him out by the scruff of the neck.

On the opposite side from where we parked was a large grassy area covered in weeds and small wild shrubs.

During late afternoons, Vangelis would play out in the undergrowth, honing his hunting skills whilst chasing bugs and butterflies. On our second evening on the beach, he came bounding back to the camper with something writhing in his mouth. It was a small rodent he'd pounced on. Claire shrieked out, and I roared out, almost knocking the table over, lunging towards a rather bemused-looking Vangelis. The tiny field mouse was still alive and very much kicking but dangling from the jaws of his tormentor. It must have been the sound of my roaring voice that caused Vangelis to drop his prey, giving Claire the chance to swoop him up and away from the diminutive rodent.

Remarkably, the mouse appeared uninjured as he scurried away at lightning speed and back towards the grass. Claire clung on to Vangelis until we were sure the mouse had made a clean getaway. With his paws firmly back on the ground, Vangelis spent ages racing around the camper, sniffing behind the wheels, searching for his evening snack. I think he was furious because shortly after giving up the search, he huffed off and went back to the grass in a big sulk.

Not long after, we had to go in search of him as it was already starting to get dark, and he hadn't returned home. I had a torch with me, and Claire had a bag of his favourite treats to lure him in. We could hear his collar bells jangling out ahead of us from behind clumps of grass, but each time we approached, he would race off in the opposite direction, stopping a few metres further behind us. He kept up this mischief for several more rounds until it was clear that we'd have to play him at his own game.

Instead of following his every move together, Claire decided to wait in one spot whilst I went in pursuit. My torch beam reflected off his beady eyes as he lay in wait ahead. Just as I got within a few feet of him, he shot out and raced past in search of another hiding place. Only this time, he ran straight into Claire, who managed to grab him before he could ruffle our feathers further.

From Bouka Beach, we continued rounding the southwestern corner of the peninsular, stopping at Foinikounta, Methoni, and Pilos and then on up the west coast. Just south of Zaharo, we found yet another nearly deserted beach and stayed several more days, enjoying the magnificent sand dunes and crashing waves. With the absence of so many other visitors we felt, at times, as if we were on a desert island, just the three of us.

It was now the third week of September, and we still wanted to return to Prespas for a fleeting visit to see our friends in Psarades and Laimos before leaving Greece. From Patras, we crossed over to Antirrio via the suspension bridge and turned left onto the national road towards Messolonghi. Eighteen miles further is the other left turn, off the main road, down to Krioneri. So we took that turn to spend a couple more days, once again, in the shadow of the mighty Varasova.

It was already quite late in the season, and we didn't expect the place to be very busy. Sure enough, there was hardly another visitor in sight as we proceeded towards the pebbly beach. Ahead of us was only one other camper parked up. It was, in fact, a large motorhome of at least eight metres in length. I didn't instantly recognise the registration number but learned later that it was from Cyprus.

As we cruised slowly past, we gave a nod and a wave to the occupants seated outside under their awning. We didn't receive any reciprocal gestures, which is a little unusual given the customary camaraderie between fellow campers and globetrotters. Regardless, we continued along the beach, putting plenty of distance between us and them to create a suitable *Vangelis Buffer Zone.*

Once parked up and settled in, we unhooked the bikes and cycled back to see our friend Christos at *Captain del Mare*. We were delighted to see him again, if only for a few days, and we spent that afternoon drinking coffee and catching up with each other's news. Fortunately, despite all the Greek government restrictions due to the COVID-19 pandemic, Christos's small family business had managed to survive intact. Greece had been particularly hard hit by state measures to control the spread of the virus, and many small businesses failed as a consequence. The pandemic had also struck the Greek economy just as it was beginning to experience moderate growth after many years of economic hardship.

As we cycled back to our camper, passing the Cypriot motorhome on the way, we noticed they were busy packing away all their stuff and preparing to leave. I gave another passing nod and wave but, as before, was met with a blank stare.

We let Vangelis out for his afternoon stroll, then set up our table and chairs outside under the awning. Moments later, I spotted our nosy-parker kitty making his way towards the Cypriot motorhome. *"We'd better go and get him back,"* said Claire. *"They don't look very friendly and might not appreciate a visit from his Lordship."*

As we started towards the Cypriots, we could see that Vangelis had almost reached their motorhome. Moments later, he was sniffing near the rear wheels and disappearing under the vehicle. We sped up just as we heard the motorhome's engine revving to life. *"Quick, they are about to leave,"* cried Claire. I was now in full gallop, waving my arms frantically to grab their attention. I couldn't see Vangelis anywhere as we reached the motorhome, only a rather annoyed face glaring at me from the cab.

"Sorry, but can you wait a moment, please? Our cat is under your motorhome," I called out. The owner didn't look one bit happy and merely replied that *the cat* would soon move once he started driving. Claire had just caught up and was down on her knees, trying to find Vangelis under the vehicle. *"I can't see him. "Oh wait, I can see him! He's sitting on the back axle."*

The Cypriot guy was still glaring at me and displaying his annoyance with us when Claire shouted, *"Got him!"* The bag of kitty treats she had been shaking had come to the rescue, and Vangelis was lured down from the axle and into her arms. It had been yet another close call.

Had the grumpy Cypriot man driven off with Vangelis clinging to the back axle, goodness knows what the outcome may have been. As we turned to walk back to the sanctuary of our camper, all we could hear was the revving engine and spinning wheels of the departing motorhome at the hands of a very disgruntled owner. He clearly wasn't having the time of his life on his Greek vacation.

This corner of Western Greece is prone to high winds that can develop very quickly. This windy phenomenon is due, in part, to the local topography and the narrow strait between Patras, on the Peloponnese side, and Antirrio on the northern coast of the Gulf of Patras.

That night, I was awakened by the sound of the wind howling past and shaking the camper in sudden, sharp bursts. Our bikes were outside, tied together but leaning close to the camper. If the wind blew hard enough, it could knock them over and cause damage. So I got up and stepped outside into the developing gale force conditions. I took extra care to gently close the habitation door behind me to ensure the wind would not get behind it and slam it shut. Inside, Vangelis was already wide awake and very curious as to why Daddy was up so early. He jumped onto the back of the couch, next to the habitation door, and stared out of the side window at me, standing in my wind-flapping pyjamas. He then jumped off the couch and leapt towards the front to stare out from behind the windscreen. During this manoeuvre, one of his large front paws must have landed and pushed the central locking system button.

A loud clunking click confirmed my worst fear. At 02:00 in the morning, I had been electronically shut outside, facing powerful winds, by my cat, who had successfully engaged the remote keyless system (RKS) from within the vehicle.

I quickly went about the task for which I had exited the camper in the first place. I unchained the bikes from the back and laid them flat on the ground. Then, I returned to the side window. I noticed that it wasn't completely locked in position, so I gently placed my hand on it and slid it open. The opening was far too small to climb up and crawl through, but I managed to put my face against it and call out Claire's name. She didn't stir because she was so fast asleep, and the howling wind must have drowned out my cry for help.

Then, without warning, I was whacked across the face by Vangelis's left paw, followed by a right hook. I pushed my arm through the window and tried to push him off the couch, but this only encouraged him to engage further in this fantastic new game that *Daddy* was playing. Every time I tried to put my face against the open window space to awaken Claire, he'd leap into action, lashing his paws at the side of the window frame in quick, deliberate, but playful bursts.

This went on for what seemed like an eternity when suddenly Claire got up to go to the loo. I let out a loud *"Claire! Quick, open the door!"* She started laughing and asked what on earth I was doing outside in such gale force conditions. I began explaining about the bikes in the wind and then getting locked out when, bam, I was thumped again by one of Vangelis's lead uppercuts. *"Just open the door, will you?"* I moaned. The door finally clicked open, and I climbed back inside to be met by my wife's titters and the continued antics of a hyper-kitten.

By early morning, the winds had eased off, and I decided to cycle to Galatas, a nearby village, for some shopping and to say goodbye to a very dear old friend.

His name is Najib, and he owns a small grocery store in the village. His store is typical of many similar mini-markets found in most Greek villages. In Greek, they are called *pantopoleío,* which translates as an e*verything for sale shop!*

In the summer of 2014, I first stepped into Najib's *pantopoleío* for some groceries. I was taken aback by how well he spoke English. The following day, I returned for more shopping and also to ask him how he knew English so well for a Greek in a small rural village. He smiled at me and said, *"I'm not Greek! I am from Syria!"*

Many years before, he had visited Greece on business from his home town of Aleppo in northern Syria. He had fallen in love with this corner of the country, (and a local girl,) and eventually married and started a family. Since that first encounter in 2014, we have remained close friends and meet at least twice a week for coffee during our visits to Krioneri. When we returned in 2015, we stayed much longer—practically eight weeks.

The day before we left that year, we went for one last brew with *the Syrian*, as he's sometimes called in the village.

Najib offered us both several small parting gifts and then took me to one side and said, with a very concerned look on his face, *"You have been here for a long time this summer without work. If you need any assistance, financially, to reach your home please ask me."*

That is our friend Najib.....*the Syrian.*

****

Chapter Seven

Prespas revisited

The journey time up to Prespas, from Krioneri, is at least six hours. It was late in the day when we finally got on the road so we stopped for the night at a small seaside town called Menidi on the Ambracian Gulf, just south of Arta.

That evening, for no particular reason, I took Vangelis's passport out of our *important documents* folder. It had been over two weeks since the vet finalised it, and I hadn't given it any scrutiny since then. As I flicked through the pages, I noticed one glaring error. Vangelis's date of birth had been entered incorrectly. The vet had written July 24th instead of June 26th. There were also other minor discrepancies that I'd learn about later, but for now, the incorrect date of birth bothered me.

Even though Vangelis had received his rabies vaccination following the recommended period, i.e. approximately nine weeks after his estimated date of birth, his passport indicated that he'd been vaccinated at only five weeks old. Would this matter? Would a sharp-eyed official at the Pet Passport Control question it? We had no idea as this, of course, was our first-ever journey with a pet on board. Nevertheless, it worried us as we didn't want any unpleasant surprises at the UK border or anywhere in between.

The following morning, we set off early for Prespas but with a slight detour. During those last few days in Krioneri, Stella often spoke about places we should visit in the Pindus mountain range, notably Vikos National

Park. It was a place we'd never been to before, and as it was only 30 miles north of Ioannina, it wasn't a massive departure from our route to Prespas. Our intention was simply to pass through, stopping maybe for one night before continuing north. As we left the city of Ioannina behind and climbed up into the higher elevations, it soon became clear that we were heading towards something quite spectacular.

Covering some 12,600 hectares (31,135 acres) of mountainous terrain, with numerous rivers, lakes, caves, deep canyons, and dense forest, we had unwittingly detoured into a hitherto unknown paradise. Best known for the giant Vikos Gorge, this area is breathtaking and an absolute paradise for hikers. The villages throughout the area look like they haven't changed in hundreds of years. They are solid square stone buildings with very narrow cobblestone streets perched on the sides of mountains.

We started in a village called Vradeto and hiked to a viewpoint called Beloi. There are breathtaking views of Vikos Gorge, which stretches over seven miles and has depths up to 1,000 metres and widths up to 2,500 metres.

Once again, we found ourselves all alone in yet another magnificent corner of Greece. We felt humbled and awed standing on the ridge of Greece's Grand Canyon! A feeling of reverence and wonder arises when you encounter something this spectacular.

By the time we hiked back to the car park next to Vradeto, it was already quite late in the day, so we decided to spend the night there.

In the fourth week of September, and at much higher elevations, the evening outdoor temperature quickly plummeted at sunset. With no other visitors around, we let Vangelis out for a romp, but he didn't stay out long.

This was his first experience in a cooler climate, and his kitten fur wasn't sufficient to keep him warm during the sudden temperature change. That evening, after we'd turned in for the night, he made numerous attempts to make the leap from the floor to our bed. After one more failed attempt, I reached down and scooped him up onto the top of our duvet cover. He curled up and, like us, fell fast asleep.

The next day, we drove to the village of Vikos and then took the narrow mountain road up to another village called Papingo, where we visited the natural rock pools. The steep road to Papingo climbs up the mountain with 16 hairpin-pin turns to navigate. Fortunately, there was very little traffic, and we could "go wide" around the bends.

On day three, we hiked along the Vjosë River (also known as the Aoös) from Konitsa. This trail starts at the iconic Konitsa stone bridge. Built in 1871, it is considered the largest single-arch stone bridge in the Balkans. In 1913, when the Turks left Konitsa, they attempted to destroy it with explosives. Fortunately, they failed, and the bridge stands strong to this day, in all its splendour.

The trail follows the Vjosë River to a narrow path that leads up another mountain to a beautiful monastery called Moni Panagias Stomiou. We couldn't believe we had never been here before or even heard of the place. This was somewhere we both felt completely relaxed and contented. We were determined to return on a future trip when we had extra time.

Our original plan to pass through the Vikos National Park had turned into four days of hiking and exploring. It was now time to continue on up to Prespas to say goodbye to our friends in Psarades and Laimos.

From Konitsa, we continued via Kefalochori to Neapoli and then on to Kastoria. We had plenty of supplies on board, so we skipped a shopping trip in Kastoria and drove the remaining 24 miles to the left turn at Trigono. This put us back onto the "one-way in and one-way out" road straight to the Prespa lakes.

We arrived back in Psarades around mid-afternoon and went to see Kiriaki and Dimitris at their small café/store. Three months had passed since our previous visit, and yet it seemed we'd only been gone for a few weeks. We sat and drank coffee with Kiriaki and Dimitris and told them about our adventures. They were particularly amused by the story of Vangelis and how a small Greek kitten had grabbed the attention of so many people from so many countries.

That evening, we went to the taverna *Ta Paragádia* for dinner and a big catch-up with Christos and Eleni. We were the only customers at the taverna; in fact, we were probably the only visitors or tourists in the whole area.

This late in the season, Psarades felt somewhat desolate and forsaken. This didn't bother us in the slightest as we were so familiar with the surroundings from so many previous visits, and we had friends here. However, a newcomer arriving for the first time might have the impression of being in a dejected and barren place.

We returned to the camper just before sunset and had to wrap up with extra layers of clothing just to sit outside with our nightcap. It was much colder than we had expected. Everything from the colour of the evening sky to the dark shadows across the mountains and forests to the murkiness of the lake below suggested that winter was just around the corner.

From our vantage point, on the opposite side of the bay, the lights of the small village twinkled as white smoke from wood-burning stoves snaked up from the old stone houses. I couldn't help but think that during the middle of winter, this village and the other small settlements dotted around the lake must feel very isolated from the rest of the world.

Claire had crocheted a small square blue woollen comforter for Vangelis to carry around in his mouth. He'd been recently picking up all kinds of debris from outside, often dumping his rubbish inside the camper, so she thought a dedicated piece of treasure might deter him. And it worked! For several days, he couldn't be parted from this small blue crocheted square, and it dangled from his mouth everywhere he went.

Up on the side of the hill, overlooking the village, he was free to come and go as he pleased. We weren't in the least bit worried about traffic dangers as there weren't any. Also, he didn't stray far from the camper as there were plenty of distractions nearby in the form of large flying insects, tiny rodents, and lizards to keep him occupied.

On one occasion, a herd of very distinctive *dwarf cows* meandered past our pitch. This shorthorn cattle breed is indigenous to the Prespa lakes and has been a part of the local culture and heritage for centuries. They, more or less, roam freely around the village of Psarades and the neighbouring villages on the Albanian side of the lake. On this occasion, they roamed freely right up to a very curious kitten sitting in the middle of their path. Vangelis didn't flinch once as the lead cow lowered her head to inspect this inquisitive little visitor. Their noses almost touched as Vangelis arched forward in sync with the cow's lowered head for a sniff at close range. He then lost interest and headed back towards us as the cows continued their amble further along and up the old French military supply trail.

Returning to this most north-westerly corner of the country involved a detour of some 285 miles. Had we just driven straight to the port of Igoumenitsa from Krioneri, the journey would have only been about three hours. But a promise is a promise, and I didn't want to leave Greece without spending a few days back in the place that had fully repaired and restored me after the anxieties and uncertainties of lockdowns and COVID restrictions.

During the five days we spent by Lake Prespa, we cycled twice back to Laimos to visit The Wise Men of the Village. They were all seated at the village café, exactly where we had last seen them three months earlier.

Old Vangelis was particularly pleased to see us again and thoroughly enjoyed all the stories I told him about our summer adventures. He roared with laughter when I acquainted him with the tale of Vangelis and the worldwide fan club that had flourished since that fateful day in Evia.

I then took my phone and showed him several of our Rocking Life on the Road Facebook posts. He was astonished at the responses. I pointed out carefully all the reactions and comments from around the world and the sheer number of post reaches, some numbering close to 100,000.

He asked if I'd also written stories about Prespas and his village. So I scrolled back to late June and early July and showed him posts from the area and the accompanying photos, comments, and positive reactions. He was very impressed and turned to his friends, seated close by, and quipped something humorous about being very famous!

Old Vangelis was born in Laimos and has spent his entire life in this village. He's a very proud man and loves his country very much, particularly this region known as Western Macedonia. He is very aware and mindful of world affairs and politics, especially in his own country, and isn't afraid to speak his mind.

At his age, he's unfamiliar with the digital era and all the latest technology, or maybe he just doesn't care about such things. He doesn't own a mobile phone or a computer, but he has a beautiful garden with abundant fruits and vegetables. Nevertheless, when he saw our Facebook posts, he clearly understood the internet's potential and effectiveness.

I also pointed out that the number of followers on our page had quadrupled over the past 12 weeks because of Vangelis, the kitty. The story had captivated thousands of folks from Western Canada to China, South Africa to Australia, New Zealand, the USA, Europe, and beyond.

"He really is a Messenger of Good News, as his name suggests," I said. Vangelis turned with a big smile and exclaimed, *"Polý Sostá,"* which translates as *"rightly said"* or *"that's correct."*

Vangelis invited us to his home again before leaving Greece to say goodbye and spend a few last moments in their company. So we agreed that in two days, we'd cycle back and call at their cottage around 10:00 in the morning. He hinted that coffee, biscuits, and maybe a drop of locally distilled Tsipouro would be proffered!

The following morning, we hiked to the Hermitage of Metamorphosis. This walk takes you through juniper and pine forests and onto the lake's shore, where you can see this amazing religious sanctuary built into the cliffs above.

It was constructed during the 13th century, when the Ottoman Empire controlled the Balkans, and also at a time when the lake's water level was much higher than it is today. Hidden from view, the Hermitage was a centre for spiritual solitude, a place of pilgrimage and prayer.

Ironically, finding myself in this former centre of spiritual solitude awakened my concerns over Vangelis's pet passport. By the time we got back to the camper, my nagging worry had developed into a generalised anxiety disorder.

Earlier that morning, we also received an email from the ferry company with important information regarding our return trip from Igoumenitsa to Ancona. All unvaccinated passengers were obliged to get tested for COVID-19 at an approved facility before boarding the vessel. It didn't offer any further information as to where we could get a rapid test done, only that it must be completed within 24 hours before the ferry's departure. It was highly unlikely that we would find an approved facility in the mountains surrounding the Prespa lakes, so I decided I needed help from our friends in the village.

Claire had a major crochet project she had to rush through that afternoon. As Vangelis had invited us to his cottage, she wanted to offer him a small, handmade parting gift. We both came up with the same idea.

A crocheted flag of Greece in the national colours of blue and white! So whilst she embarked on this latest crochet challenge I cycled down to see Eleni at her taverna *Ta Paragádia*.

She had plenty of friends and contacts in Florina, and if anyone could help find a COVID test centre, it would be her. After explaining this latest travel requirement, she phoned a friend who worked at a pharmacy in Florina. A test could be done at the hospital in Florina, but, of course, this was of little use to us as the test results were needed within the 24 hours preceding our departure. Further inquiries revealed that two pharmacies in Igoumenitsa offered COVID rapid tests for a fee of 10 euros per person. No pre-booking was necessary; just show up for the swabbing and forfeit 20 euros in total.

With that box ticked, my next concern was Vangelis's passport. Eleni suggested that vets in Igoumenitsa might be more familiar with all the requirements concerning the transport of pets because of the number of tourists travelling to and from the port. It was sound advice, but I really needed confirmation sooner, as Igoumenitsa was our last stop before we left Greece. I thanked Eleni for all her help and then called to see Kiriaki at her café. The following day would be our last full day in Psarades, and I wanted to make sure she and Dimitris would be around so we could say goodbye. I also wanted to stock up on the best honey I've ever tasted.

Locally produced and stocked at Kiriaki's store is an assortment of fantastic *bio-honeys.* There's thick, dark oak honey, almost resin-like, with rich antioxidant and antibacterial properties. The bees, I was told, collect a fluid that trickles directly from acorns to produce this variety. It has a wonderfully deep, rich, and malty taste. Then there's forest honey made from resins and sugary substances that the bees gather from forest trees. It has stronger and more intense malty flavours. Another favourite of mine is pine honey, which comes from the honeydew that bees gather directly on the conifers. It has a dark amber colour and a fantastic sweet and spicy taste and fragrance. All are available at Kiriaki's village store.

We chatted for several hours over coffee, taking turns to speak in English and then Greek; that way, both of us would listen, converse, and learn.

Kiriaki is very positive, cheerful, and optimistic. She was very reassuring when I told her about my niggling concerns over the pet passport and travelling back to the UK with the famous kitty.

We agreed to meet up the following afternoon to say goodbye, and with a takeaway coffee balanced in one hand for Claire, I cycled back up the hill to the camper.

Just as I reached the top, I passed three young girls out for a late afternoon stroll. Ahead was the large open area where we were parked, and crossing from one side to the other was Vangelis clutching the blue crocheted comforter in his mouth.

Claire sat outside, overlooking the village, making fine progress with her Greek flag. I handed over the coffee and brought her up to speed on the prospects and possibilities of COVID lateral flow tests at pharmacies in Igoumenitsa.

"Have you seen Vangelis?" she asked. *"He's been playing here all afternoon with that piece of wool I made for him."* I told her I'd just seen him dandering to the opposite side of the parking area with the aforementioned woolly

comforter in his mouth. I also mentioned the three girls whom I'd passed on my bike. I turned and walked around the camper, and sure enough, the girls were on the far side, sitting on a wall, with Vangelis in full entertainment mode. I waved over and loudly informed them of his name. This was to signal that he wasn't a stray or a lost kitten and that he did have a home in case they thought otherwise. They giggled at the name, waved back, and continued playing with Vangelis, who thoroughly enjoyed all this latest attention.

As Claire was very busy with her current vocation in vexillology, it was up to me to prepare the evening meal. Inside the camper, I buckled down to the task at hand, oblivious to what was or wasn't going on outside. With a pan sizzling and a pot bubbling, I glanced out of the kitchen window, expecting to see the three girls still playing with Vangelis. But there wasn't anyone there. I crossed the parking area to the wall where they had been playing, then ran to the top of the road and looked down the hill. There was no sign of them at all and no sign of Vangelis. My heart sank once again.

Claire instinctively understood something was wrong and was by my side as I turned around. *"Let's split up and search the area,"* she commanded. I walked along by the bushes, next to the steep descent down to the lake, whilst Claire searched up the old military path. We then scouted around the other side next to the camper. Beside the wall, I found Vangelis's blue comforter lying in the grass. The sight of it only increased my uneasiness and worry. We were only a day away from leaving Prespas and only a few days away from leaving Greece.

Suddenly, I realised that a pot and pan were still on the heat back in the camper. I rushed inside to be met by the acrid, bitter reek of burnt onions from the pan and clouds of steam gushing from the pot. How quickly it can all go belly up.

Back outside, I grabbed my bicycle and cycled down the hill to see if there was any sign of him. Meanwhile, Claire, shaking a bag of cat treats, headed off again to comb the surrounding area. From the top of the hill to the bottom is approximately 500 metres. I went down about halfway, very slowly, whilst calling out his name. Trees, brambles, and thick undergrowth are on either side of the single-track road. If Vangelis had been hiding in there, finding him wouldn't have been impossible.

My gut feeling told me that he was somewhere close by the camper, so I gave up where I was and cycled back. Claire met me with a worried look on her face. Vangelis was still absent without leave.

We quickly went over the chain of events, from the three girls arriving and playing with Vangelis to when I realised he was missing. The time frame could not have been more than twenty minutes. *"Do you think he followed those girls back to Psarades?"* Claire asked. For a 12-week-old kitten, the distance down the hill and onto the village would most likely be too much. However, he had followed the German couple that evening in Krioneri. *"Maybe he followed them so far and then gave up?"* Claire continued.

I went inside, grabbed the red cat box, tied it to the back of my bicycle, and set off again down the hill. Before leaving, I told Claire to keep her phone handy. If I did find him, I would most likely need help getting back up with the additional *baggage* in hand.

I slowly re-descended the narrow road, glancing from left to right while listening out for the tinkle of his collar bells. At the bottom of the hill, a sharp turn veers to the left before descending further down to a wide, open, flat area. On this corner, off to the left-hand side, lies a large pile of small rocks and rubble. The remains of old walls that once separated villagers' gardens back when the lake level was much higher.

As I made the swooping turn, I heard the distinctive sound of a bell tinkle. I screeched to a halt, dismounted, and scoured the rocky ground off to my left. I couldn't believe my eyes. Straight ahead, standing on top of the discarded stones and rubble, was Vangelis. A wave of euphoria swept over me as I clambered over the rocks, with cat box in hand, calling out his name. He did not attempt to hide or play games. Instead, he came running toward me, oblivious to the panic he had just caused. Once safe and secure inside the red box, I called Claire on my phone. *"I've got him!"* I sighed, *"But I'll need your help to get back up."*

Claire cycled down and carried the red box whilst I pushed the two bicycles back up the hill. At the camper, Vangelis was immediately confined inside whilst we abandoned any notion of cooking an evening meal and headed back to Psarades for dinner at Eleni and Christos's taverna.

Reflecting later on this latest disappearing act, we both agreed that Vangelis must have followed the girls down the hill. Then, most likely, at the bottom of the track, he became disorientated and confused. It was certainly the longest distance he'd travelled to date, and we were adamant that he wouldn't be free to roam anywhere again until we were safely back home on the Isle of Man.

We cycled to Laimos the next morning to visit Vangelis and Magdalena as planned. They were delighted with the crocheted Greek flag that Claire had completed in record time. We sat outside in the cool morning air as the sun appeared just above the tree line.

It was early October, and everyone was dressed appropriately for the cooler conditions. I was wearing my long track pants with a fleece jacket and a woolen beanie hat on my head. And, for the first time in months, I had socks and shoes on my feet. The summer season was a short one in these parts.

Magdalena had prepared an assortment of homemade cookies, jams, and delicious Greek coffee. Predictably, a bottle of locally distilled Tsipouro shortly appeared, and Vangelis, Claire, and I gulped down a shot of this early morning snifter with a loud "*Yiamas!*"

Magdalena declined the Tsipouro tasting ceremony and hastened back and forth from her kitchen, bringing out additional biscuits and preserved fruits. Then small gifts appeared. There was a small box with eggs from their chickens, a bag containing several tomatoes, and a cucumber with sprigs of rosemary and oregano tossed in for good measure. We were experiencing, once again, Greek *"filoxenía"* at its finest and how we appreciated every moment.

In a matter of days, we'd be far away from these idyllic and rural surroundings, facing hectic, stressful, dense traffic and congestion, all the way back to the UK. Here in Prespas, we were worlds apart from the hustle and bustle of motorways, cities and crowds, the noises, the rush hours and peak hours, and the fuss and furore of modern life. We hugged Vangelis and Magdalena, said our goodbyes, and thanked them again for their kindness and hospitality. Old Vangelis smiled and repeated the words: *"Never forget, the door to my home is always open to you and Claire."*

And with that, we cycled out of Laimos for the last time that year and along the road towards the Koula, up the side of the mountain, past the small church of Ágios Geórgios, and down the other side into Psarades.

It had turned into a beautiful sunny morning, with the outside temperature almost hitting a scorching high of nearly 16 degrees! What a difference compared to Athens, Patras, and Messolonghi, where daytime highs were still around 24 - 25 degrees.

Sleepy-eyed, Vangelis was waiting for us behind the camper's habitation door. As soon as I opened the door, he casually brushed past me, his tail in the air, to head outdoors. But I was one step ahead. With one swoop, I had him in my grasp and held him securely while Claire slipped on the harness. He could go outside, but from now on, it would only be with his harness and a very secure tether attached.

Before leaving, we still had to see Christos, Eleni, Kiriaki, Dimitris, and Germanos and his family, so around mid-afternoon, we headed down to the village.

The plan was to get on the road at around 07:30 in the morning and drive towards the coast. It had been worth our while to return once more to Prespas before leaving the country. Not only to see our friends but to see the place in a different light, in colder weather conditions,

185

and understand how desolate it must be during the darkest months of winter.

The following morning, just as the sun was rising, we set off out of Psarades, up and down the mountainside, out to the main road, and towards Kastoria. We didn't encounter another vehicle until we reached the outskirts of town.

On our way, Claire made a long shopping list. Our food supplies had dwindled, and we needed to stock up on everything from pasta to gas. I navigated across town towards the supermarket we had used earlier in the summer on our way down to Evia. And just like the previous visit, I turned onto the same dusty, potholed truck stop to park. Claire grabbed her shopping list and a trolley token and disappeared into the supermarket, leaving me to keep Vangelis company.

For the following few moments, I sat glancing at the map, estimating the time and distance to the port of Igoumenitsa. We only had to call there briefly to check out a pharmacy where we could get a COVID rapid lateral flow test done. Then with the remaining few days, until the ferry departure, we could relax along the coast just south of Igoumenitsa.

There was also the issue of Vangelis's passport. We had to find a veterinary surgeon to check that out. I got up to fetch a bottle of water from the fridge and, after taking a slug, returned to the driver's seat that Vangelis had quickly occupied. I shooed him off, sat down, looked out the window, and spotted something quite astonishingly remarkable!

With marbled front steps and a clean, shining shop front, plants adorning either side of the doorway was a veterinary clinic! The same one we had parked outside three months earlier. The same one that looked almost out of place next to the dusty, potholed truck stop.

I rubbed my eyes and looked again. Above the doorway was a green sign and, in large lettering, the word Κτηνίατρος *(Ktiníatros)*, meaning veterinary surgeon.

I jumped out of my seat and put Vangelis into the red cat box before grabbing a notepad and scribbling a message to Claire. I stuck the note to the front door window, and then, with his passport in hand, I left the camper and walked straight up to those marbled front steps.

Sitting behind a desk in the corner, a young man was shuffling paperwork with a phone wedged between his ear and right shoulder. I gently closed the door and waited while he finished his conversation. *"Yassas! My name is Apostolis; how can I help you?"* he asked, getting up from behind his desk. I held the red box out in front of me and blurted out:

"Inside this box is Vangelis, and we are leaving for Ancona, Italy, in a few days, but I think his pet passport might have a problem, and I am worried about the pet control authorities in France, at the port of Calais, for travel to the UK and onwards to the Isle of Man. I am from Ireland, but...."

The vet raised his hand to politely interrupt me and, with a puzzled look, asked, *"Who or what is Vangelis, and where are you travelling to?"* He was now smiling at the box because two beady eyes were staring back at him from behind the grid hatch. *"Ah! Vangelis is a cat! Let's have a look at him."*

I followed him to a screened-off area with a large metal veterinary table. I opened the door of the pet carrier, and Vangelis stepped out and stretched onto the table. *"Oh, he is a very handsome boy!"* exclaimed Apostolis. *"And what huge paws he has. I think we are in the presence of a tiger kitten here."*

He then proceeded with a full routine check-up, starting with a stethoscope placed on Vangelis's left side to check his pulse. Then he folded back one ear, glanced inside, and gave it a quick sniff. Up next were his teeth and gums, followed by his nose.

The novelty of new surroundings was slowly wearing off, and by the time Apostolis started a body check for any lumps or bumps, Vangelis began to fume. Finally came a temperature check, which was the final indignity, using a thermometer inserted into the opposite end of his body. He turned angrily and tried to bite his hand off, but I managed to intervene, which, more or less, concluded the health check.

Throughout the examination, I acquainted Apostolis with Vangelis's remarkable story, which included full details about his increasing worldwide fame and international fan club. The fact that he had been in Evia only days before the northern half of the island went up in flames reminded us both of the awful carnage left in the wake of the summer wildfires. Apostolis spoke not only of the extensive damage to homes and infrastructure but also of the huge loss to livestock, pets, and wild animals.

Back at his desk, he opened the EU pet passport and started flicking through the pages. After a few moments, he spotted the discrepancy between the date of birth and the rabies vaccination date. He also pointed out that the declaration: *Animal is fit to be transported for the intended journey* had been omitted. Furthermore, the *Description of Animal* and *Marking of Animal* sections should have been sealed with a tamper-proof, clear plastic film.

While Apostolis was busy correcting, amending, and endorsing the passport, I stepped outside to see if there was any sign of Claire. Just as I was about to return inside, I saw her struggling with a large shopping trolley across the dusty, potholed truck stop. I ran to help and excitedly told her my stroke of luck with the passport, pointing to the small clinic with the marbled front steps. I promptly explained how Apostolis was righting the wrongs as we spoke.

"That's great news," she said. *"Now, let's sort this lot out so we can go together and get Vangelis and meet our hero vet!"*

We ditched all the shopping inside the camper, hastily returned the trolley, and headed up the marbled front steps. Inside, Apostolis was finishing the passport amendments while simultaneously conducting a heated conversation over the phone and banging his hand loudly on the desk.

This scenario is quite common throughout the Balkans and especially in Greece. It doesn't suggest, for a moment, that there is a dispute or a row in progress. It could simply mean that he's discussing a romantic dinner with his girlfriend or that his Mum has just invited him for coffee and cake on Sunday. In fact, it's not uncommon in Greece to see friends yelling at each other in public, wildly gesticulating, only to shake hands, embrace, and high-five each other immediately after.

As soon as Apostolis concluded his phone conversation, he stood up, smiled at us, and said, *"Sorry, that was my sister on the phone. We're meeting with friends this evening; it's her birthday today."*

He then picked up the blue EU pet passport from his desk, handed it to me, and said, *"All is well. Now you will have no problems."* We could barely express our gratitude and thanked him profusely for all his help. Vangelis was still in the box, resting on one of the chairs next to the desk. Claire went to retrieve him as I turned to ask Apostolis how much we owed for everything.

He looked at the box with Vangelis staring out, then at me, then at Claire, and calmly announced, *"For Vangelis, no charge, to bring him luck!"* Once again, we were on the receiving end of a highly concentrated dose of Greek *filoxenia*, and we knew it would be futile to protest this kind and thoughtful gesture.

As we stepped outside into the late morning sunshine, Apostolis wished us a *"Kaló taxídi"* and said, *"This is a very good thing that you do, giving Vangelis a home."* I shook his hand and replied, *"Animals have a purpose when they come into our lives."*

Time was already creeping on, and we were both feeling quite peckish, so we left Vangelis to settle down inside the camper and headed into the town for one last visit to find a gyros snack bar.

****

Metsovo is a winter ski resort town a little over halfway between Kastoria and Igoumenitsa. It was nearly midday when we got on the road, so we decided to look for a stopover somewhere near Metsovo and continue to the coast the following day.

Our journey took less than two hours, and upon arrival, I followed Claire's instructions to a camper stopover that she had found on her *Park4Night* app. It was, apparently, just north of Metsovo, but we simply couldn't locate it. The directions would have taken us off-road and down a dusty trail adjacent to a forest. So we gave up searching and started to look for a suitable stopover using our own well-honed, razor-sharp intuition in such matters.

We passed a car park next to a row of large green rubbish bins, but it was on a slope and unsuitable for an overnight stay. A large motorhome was parked next to the bins, and as we passed, I noticed that the registration was Romanian.

A short distance further along, we turned down a narrow road and found a suitable parking area next to the roadside. There was open, hilly, undulating countryside on one side and a forest on the other. As soon as I switched off the engine, Vangelis started making a big fuss to go outside. So I put his harness on and, with a long leash attached, took him for a walk amongst the trees.

By now, he was getting much more used to the harness and didn't mind going on a guided tour of the area with me. However, it was more a case of me accompanying him, as any attempt to direct him in any particular direction was met with a tantrum. He had perfected his very own unique method of disapproval and protested by lying on the ground, refusing to budge.

After about twenty minutes amongst the trees, I picked him up and returned to the narrow road. From there, we walked back to the camper.

Claire was sitting outside chatting with a woman and her young daughter. They were from Romania, and it was their motorhome we had passed earlier. They had been out for a stroll and stopped to say hello. Both mum and daughter could speak perfect English, and were regular visitors to this corner of Greece. Once again, Vangelis took centre stage, and they were fascinated by his story and online celebratory status.

We chatted for the remainder of the afternoon and discovered that their motorhome was, in fact, their full-time home. They had left Romania to escape the ongoing COVID restrictions in that country and had no immediate plans to return. The young daughter's name was Irina, and she must have only been about nine years old and home-schooled by her mum.

When I talked about my online posts and how the story of Vangelis had reached many people worldwide, bringing lots of joy with it, they fully grasped the meaning. Irina said, *"Too many people are sad about the pandemic, and I think this happy kitten story cheers them up."*

And there it was in a nutshell. Out of the mouths of babes! I didn't need to elaborate on the origins and meaning of the name Vangelis either. They immediately grasped it and agreed that a *Messenger of Good News* was a worthy attribute.

We were up and away early the following morning and reached Igoumenitsa around 10:00 am. It's a busy coastal city, bustling with activity, and parking anywhere near the centre is nigh impossible. So we stopped on the outskirts and walked in.

Of course, our only business in town was the obligatory COVID lateral flow tests and where we could get them done. The first pharmacy we called at didn't offer the service but was able to direct us to one of only two in town that did.

Inside, an assistant confirmed that the test was a Greek government requirement that had to be carried out within the preceding 24 hours before travel and cost 10 euros each. The test results would be made available almost immediately, and a paper copy and email would be provided. No appointment was needed; just show up and prepare to have your nostrils swabbed.

We were now into the second week of October and still had a couple of days remaining until our ferry to Ancona on October 11th. So we re-confirmed the pharmacy's opening times, double-checked that no appointment was needed, and left. We'd return on the day of departure and get our tests done well within the 24-hour time frame.

From Igoumenitsa, we headed south, along the coast road, towards the port city of Preveza. The first time we visited Greece together was in the summer of 2009, twelve years earlier. We had travelled along the same coast road back then and stopped off at a small, charming seaside village called Mitikas.

From this village extends the longest beach in Europe. For 14 miles, this wide, sandy beach, named *Monolithi*, runs all the way back to the village of Kastrosikia. The name comes from a large single rock that once projected up from the sea to a height of over ten metres. Mono *Μόνος*, which means single, and Lithos *Λίθος*, meaning stone, hence *Monolithi!*

Unfortunately, the large rock was destroyed during the Second World War by German and Italian troops who used it for target practice for their mortar rounds. Today, the remains of the *Monolithi* rock are hidden underwater and serve as a very shallow reef.

We decided it would be a fitting end to our Greek odyssey to spend our last few days and nights parked next to this beautiful sandy beach with its large crashing waves rolling in from the Ionian Sea.

There are plenty of places to park along the beach road, and freshwater showers are available every 200-300 metres. We found a hard-packed, sandy area with trees on either side.

During the afternoon, we received warning SMS messages to our phones from the Greek government forecasting severe weather and possible flooding in the area over the next 48 hours. That first night, there was nothing more than a strong breeze blowing, but the following night, the heavens opened, and the wind roared. Our camper was shaking like a leaf on a tree, and we started to get very concerned by the sheer amount of rainwater lashing the ground.

I shone a torch from one of the side windows and could see mini-lakes forming all around us. The ground we were parked on may have been hard-packed when we arrived, but with the torrential rain, it would soon turn soft and sinky. We had to move fast.

Vangelis was fast asleep throughout the stormy weather, but I had to wake him up and move him off the driver's seat to swivel it around and move it to the forward position. We turned onto the beach road and drove down to where it widens up into a broad and spacious parking area. We were on solid asphalt now and pointed into the wind. We all went back to bed and managed to sleep until daybreak.

We woke up to the clatter of Vangelis leaping from one side of the cab window to the other. I peered from under the duvet to see him clawing and jumping nervously at the windscreen. Something was annoying him, so I got up to see what was wrong. The source of his jitters was the rainfall, or raindrops, to be more precise.

Outside, beads of rain rolled slowly down the windscreen, twisting and turning in different directions, sending Vangelis into a frenzy as he tried to catch and stop each and every droplet.

"Come and take a look at this," I called out to Claire. We stood there, bursting with laughter at his antics, when it suddenly dawned on us both that this was the first rainfall any of us had witnessed all summer. *"This must be the first time he's ever seen rain,"* Claire said. And it was true. Since our arrival in Greece at the end of June, we had only experienced sunny, blue skies and soaring temperatures.

By late afternoon, the stormy weather had passed us by, and the sun shone again. I unfolded our camp chairs and table outside, sat down and updated our Facebook travel blog. I had all the latest news about Vangelis's visit to the vet in Kastoria and his recently updated pet passport to report.

Apart from a few locals who had arrived for swims, we were very much alone on *Monolithi* beach. We weren't taking any chances with Vangelis, who was firmly attached to his tether. This didn't bother him, and as soon as he spotted Claire's empty chair, he jumped on it.

She had been inside, gathering up her crochet, when her seat had been repossessed. But instead of shooing him off, she took photographs for my post because he looked so happy, chilled out, and content.

As the waves crashed along the shore and the sun sank lower in the sky, he sat with partly closed eyes, his neck arched back, sniffing the gentle breeze, occasionally glancing left and right up and down the beach.

It was almost as if he knew he'd be leaving his native Greece very soon and had to take it all in and enjoy these last glimpses.

****

Chapter Eight

The Road Home

On the morning of October 12th, we drove the one-hour journey back to Igoumenitsa for the obligatory COVID lateral flow tests. Our ferry departure was scheduled for midnight that evening, but we wanted to get the tests done, dusted, and out of the way.

We returned to the same pharmacy, had our nostrils swabbed, and were promptly informed of negative test results. We were also promptly separated from 20 euros for the service.

We then drove to the ferry terminal to double-check that our sailing was on time and to show our negative test results to the check-in staff. Claire remained with Vangelis while I crossed the car park towards the large terminal building.

There were loads of people milling about everywhere, many appeared to have no particular purpose or direction. Whole families were randomly scattered along the pedestrian areas and curbsides, sitting on huge ornate blankets that had been flung on the ground. Women, wrapped in colourful flowered print kaftans, prepared food over single gas stoves whilst bare-footed kids ran hazardously in all directions. Their menfolk stood nearby in small groups, chain-smoking cigarettes, gesticulating and bickering. All the men wore ill-fitting single-breasted jackets over brown polo-neck sweaters. There was a flowery, earthy, woody kind of fragrance with a zingy tang of cumin and other spices permeating the air.

I wasn't 100% certain of ethnicity, but it felt like I'd stumbled into the final days of the Ottoman Empire.

Inside the terminal building, two bored-looking female employees sat behind the Anek information window, chatting to themselves. I waited several moments before one turned to engage in customer services. It seemed like an effort for her to perform the job description.

There was next to zero interest when I enquired about our ferry sailing. *"Maybe you check back later, maybe the ship is delayed, maybe not, who knows?"* came the reply as she turned to continue chit-chatting with her colleague whilst filing her long manicured nails.

I then produced our negative COVID test results, expecting some kind of verification, but there was only complete apathy, bordering on disregard. I started to get the sinking feeling that I was out of pocket, to the tune of 20 euros, for a worthless piece of paper that nobody was interested in.

Back outside, I zigzagged my way to the camper through the miniature version of Ancient Constantinople that had manifestly increased in size during my brief visit to the terminal. Several battered old white vans had arrived and double parked nearby, with a steady stream of men, women, and children exiting from the rear doors and making their way to the encampment.

For no particular reason, I began to reflect on the word *van*. I wondered if it was a contraction of the word *caravan?* After all, the word *caravan* can be traced back to the Persian *kārwān* and the Arabic *qaīrawān,* meaning a group of desert travellers. The 15th-century French word *caravane* also refers to a large group of people, typically traders and pilgrims, travelling together towards a pre-determined destination.

I pondered the etymology of the word van all the way back to our own van, where I spotted Vangelis staring from behind the front window of....... the van!

Then it occurred to me that the three of us were also like a 15th-century *caravane,* travelling together towards a pre-determined destination.

"How did you get on?" asked Claire, glancing up from her crocheting. (In itself, a needlework technique, shrouded in mystery, widely believed to have originated in Arabia, where it spread along Arab *qaīrawān* routes to other parts of the known world.)

I told her about the blasé check-in staff in the terminal building and their disinterest in our COVID test results and suggested we leave the port area and find a quieter place to park.

On the way into Igoumenitsa earlier that day, I had spotted a picnic area on the left-hand side, set back from the road overlooking the port. It was only about 10 minutes out of town and a much more suitable location to spend the rest of our time before check-in. We got our table and chairs out, and Vangelis climbed up trees securely tethered to a nearby bench.

My Facebook travel blog post from the previous afternoon had already garnered nearly 30,000 reaches with hundreds of reactions and dozens of heartwarming comments from all over the world:

"Hope you have a wonderful trip back, all three of you!"

"Hola from Espana! I'm sure you will get Vangelis home as long as all documents are in order."

"His wonderful story has moved everyone, and I'm sure everyone has their fingers crossed. I wish you an uneventful journey back."

"I hope he will stay safe with you. You all deserve a happy ending to this incredible journey."

"Greetings from Massachusetts! What a beautiful kitty. Safe travels back home."

Amongst all of these uplifting and positive remarks were several that were somewhat less enthusiastic. A few *social media experts* weighed in with their unbridled knowledge of pet vaccinations, microchipping, and health certification.

Comments like *"he needs his rabies jab three weeks before entering the UK"* and *"he needs to be wormed five days before arrival"* were just downright wrong. Such erroneous remarks were anything but helpful. We were confident that we'd followed all the rules and regulations and, with Apostolis's help, Vangelis's passport was in order.

Nevertheless, the problem with other people's opinions is that sometimes they can plant small seeds of doubt. In this case, it had been the words *"needs to be wormed five days before arrival"* that had activated the anxiety neurotransmitters in my brain's amygdala, setting off a temporary bout of irrational worry. But we had really no reason to believe any dubious advice from *online experts* and every reason to ignore it, which is exactly what we did, after all things considered.

We left the picnic area in the late afternoon and drove back down to the port. Traffic around the terminal building had increased so much that looking for a parking space was pointless. Instead, we turned down one of the side streets and found a place not far from an authentic-looking Greek taverna. The sudden inclination to eat out instead of cooking in the camper was mutual. It also seemed very appropriate as it was our last night in Greece.

A plate of char-grilled souvlaki skewers with fried potato chips and a Greek *horiátiki* salad hit the spot, as did the cold Mythos beer.

After dinner, we headed over to the passport and check-in control. On the dockside of the ferry terminal, the extensive wharf provides plenty of space for waiting vehicles. And with plenty of spare time, joining the queue on the departure side made sense rather than hanging around in a narrow street.

At check-in, we were told that the incoming ferry was late and to expect at least a one to two-hour delay. This came as absolutely no surprise to us. The ferry services between Italy and Greece are notorious for their tardiness. And their punctuality, or lack thereof, perfectly compliments the crummy services on board.

After flicking through our passports, the port police wanted to look inside the camper. We had already put Vangelis in his red box and placed him in an open space overhead the cab in full view of the anticipated vehicle inspection. It was already pitch dark, and the cop had to shine a torch around the inside, opening up a few cupboards before pointing his beaming light straight into

Vangelis's face. There wasn't any request to show the pet passport, and no questions were asked.

From the check-in positions, we drove along the brightly lit wharf, looking for some kind of signage to indicate where we should park and wait. There weren't any signs, and there were none of the usual port operatives in high-viz vests pointing the way. So we just pulled over behind several lines of parked vehicles and confirmed with other passengers that we were, indeed, in the right queue for the phantom ferry.

The sailing duration between Igoumenitsa and Ancona is approximately 19 hours. We booked a cabin on board and packed a shopping bag with sandwiches, snacks, and bottled water. We had no intention of paying the galactic prices in the ferry's cafeteria.

We hadn't booked onboard pet accommodation for Vangelis because we felt that he would be more comfortable and content left inside the camper in familiar surroundings. Nevertheless, it meant he would be on his own throughout the crossing, the most extended period of separation since we had been together.

To ensure he would sleep for most of the journey, I took him outside, with his harness and leash attached, for a long walk along the harbour. Meanwhile, Claire filled his pet dish with extra food and left several bowls of water out for him.

The delayed incoming ferry docked around 01:30, followed by the usual chaotic scenes of revving engines and prepping for the impending stampede. Queue jumping, near misses, and lots of pushing and shoving aren't uncommon. Uniformed officials yell and shout at impatient drivers and occasionally at each other. Lots of whistles shriek, and many horns honk during these periods of pandemonium. It was just another example of a classic, disorderly, disorganised, and poorly regulated embarkation at a Greek port.

When it was our turn to drive up the main ramp into the belly of the boat, a dude in a small car to the rear astonishingly managed to overtake us at speed, spin 180 degrees, and then race up the inside ramp to the upper deck. The intensity of boarding a Greek ferry has the potential to provoke a nasty skin disease from all the stress.

Once on board, we made our way up steep stairwells to the upper decks where the accommodation was situated. The deck was a labyrinth of narrow corridors, crisscrossing each other, leading to blocks of cabins. A few other exhausted travellers, pulling their cases and bags and panting through tight-fitting blue face masks, struggled to match cabin numbers on their tickets to actual cabins amidst this network of rabbit warrens. We didn't fare any better and several times took wrong turns, having to navigate our way back past fellow disorientated passengers.

Finally, we found our allotted crib for the night, shoved the paper key into the slot, waited for a tiny indicator to flash green, pushed the door open, and stumbled inside.

"I'm not moving another inch from here for the next 18 hours," Claire gasped. And I couldn't have agreed more. I threw myself onto the lower bunk while Claire went to check out the shower and loo. Then, behind the washroom door, I heard her muffled voice say, *"The toilet's broken." "What do you mean, the toilet's broken?"*

I replied. *"Well, it doesn't flush, and there's no water coming out."*

I got up and pushed down on the large button atop the cistern. The toilet's bowl wheezed and gasped for a few seconds, suggesting that it was, indeed, malfunctioning. This meant I had to go back through the maze of corridors and search for the information desk. I left fully conscious that my journey would most likely be in vain. And sure enough, after making my way to the reception area, I saw several other passengers complaining about the same problem ahead of me.

When it was my turn in the queue, I approached the desk where the most perfectly polished and highly maintained stewardess I'd ever seen greeted me with a dazzling, ruby red-lipped smile. I only managed the words *"the toilet in our cabin is....."* when, with a wave of her manicured nails, she sliced through my words with a simple but firm *"I know."* She then completely blanked me and summoned the next waiting passenger.

It was rumored, amongst the disgruntled, that the entire cabin deck we were on, had developed a problem with the plumbing and it wouldn't be fixed until the ferry docked in Ancona. This meant the only alternative was to use the public toilets in the ship's cafés and bars.

I turned around and headed back to our cabin, leaving behind a cacophony of protest from the other passengers. I didn't see the point in complaining. It's difficult enough finding a plumber on land during normal working hours, let alone in the middle of the Adriatic Sea at 2:00 in the morning.

The ferry crossing was not the smoothest we'd ever experienced. Several times during the night, we were jolted wide awake by the eerie sounds of the ship's hull heaving, flexing, and pitching in the rough sea. Our thoughts went out instinctively to our little travel buddy, all alone in the camper, many decks below. With car decks strictly off-limits at sea, we could only hope he was settled and safe and not stressing out over this long stretch of isolation.

Due to the two-hour delay leaving Igoumenitsa, the ferry didn't dock in Ancona until around 6:00 p.m. I left Claire in the cafeteria and went out onto the upper deck to watch our arrival into the port, which appears to resemble an elbow jutting out into Adriatic.

It was dark outside, with drizzle in the air and felt much cooler. The sight of bright harbour lights and busy flashing beacons, gantry cranes, and freight containers stacked high brought me back down to earth with a bang.

We were back in a world of concrete and steel, motorways and congestion, shopping malls and industrial zones. It was a world where you could feel very detached very quickly.

Just then, the ship's tannoy chimed, followed by instructions for all vehicle drivers and their passengers to return to the car decks. I dashed back to the cafeteria, where Claire was waiting, and from there, we descended the stairwells, making our way back to the camper.

Just behind the habitation door we were met by a very animated and overjoyed Vangelis. He made such a fuss at seeing us again and it was very clear that separation anxieties had been mutual. I checked his dishes and there was was still plenty of food and water remaining. Then Claire spotted something next to his litter tray. *"Oh look, the poor little guy has been seasick,"* she said. The rolling and pitching of the ferry had clearly unsettled him during the long hours.

All around us, there were the clanking sounds of chains being dragged from trucks, doors slamming, alarms and bells sounding. Before we knew it, there was movement ahead, and we were quickly instructed to start our engine and drive back down the steep ramp to the lower deck.

We exited the stern of the ship into a bleak, rainy evening and followed the directions out of the port and into the flow of city traffic. There were no checks, controls or delays, and we soon picked up the main road towards the A14 autostrada, also known as the "Adriatic motorway."

In the back of the camper, Vangelis was unusually very agitated. Since leaving the port, he hadn't settled down at all, loudly protesting and constantly jumping from one side to the other.

The traffic en route was heavy, fast-moving, and chaotic. Then, after a few miles, the rain developed into a steady downpour, slamming against the windscreen, forcing us to slow right down as the wiper blades struggled to cope with the deluge. Added to this were dazzling headlights, taillights, flashing brake lights, and indicators, making driving conditions much more hazardous. It all felt a million miles away from the peace and tranquillity of the Greek mountains and villages.

We kept on driving for at least another three or four hours until we reached a small town called Soragna. It's just northwest of Parma and has a free camper stop where we have stayed several times in the past. There are enough spaces for at least a dozen campers, but ours was the only one parked there on that wet and miserable night.

The rain had eased off enough for me to take a short stroll around the block. Vangelis came along, safely attached to his lead, and I think even he was feeling the change in weather and scenery. It probably explained why he had been so flustered on the drive out of Ancona.

The excessive noisy traffic, in the pouring rain, in darkness and after a long and lonely 19-hour ferry trip must have bewildered him.

The next morning, we were up early and away towards Piacenza, and from there, we took the A1 autostrada to Alessandria.

There were still uncertainties about travelling north via Switzerland if you were an unvaccinated British citizen. I didn't want to risk any health security hassles over Claire's passport with twitchy Swiss border police. So we took the same route that we'd taken to reach Ancona in June. Only in the opposite direction!

We reached Alessandria around one in the afternoon and, after a bite to eat, motored on via Turin to reach the very expensive Fréjus tunnel connecting Italy to France via the Cottian Alps. After eight miles through the tunnel, we were back in the Auvergne-Rhône-Alpes region, and once again, our pockets were 62 euros lighter after paying the sky-high tunnel toll charge.

We found a free camper stop near Chambéry and stayed the night. It had been a full day's drive from Soragna, and we were still less than halfway to Calais.

Our Eurotunnel shuttle was scheduled for the following Sunday afternoon, so we still had plenty of time to reach Calais. The next day was Thursday, and we set off bright and early towards Lyon, then Dijon, Nancy and Metz.

The plan was to return to the *Camping Bon Accueil* in Alzingen, Luxembourg, for two nights. It had been an absolute joy to stay on this campsite, with its neat little hedges, on the journey down. It had also been our trip's first milestone, leaving us confident of a smooth onward journey. So it seemed like the perfect end to our adventures to return there for a few days.

Well, it was not to be. On arrival, the whole place looked shut down and deserted. I stepped out to investigate and noticed that the barrier blocking the main entrance was secured with a heavy padlock, and the office door displayed a *Fermé-Geschlossen* sign. *"Always check the evidence,"* I said to Claire on my return to the camper, *"The place is shut, fermé and definitely geschlossened."*

We let the air of disappointment linger for a few moments before Claire announced, *"Right! We'll have to go somewhere else then."* And with that we motored on and found another campsite, much closer to the city, just off a conjested dual carriageway with a very busy road junction.

Once again, upon arrival, we were met by an imposing entry-exit security barrier. Claire left to find the reception area and check-in. When she came back, she was waving a small, white plastic card in her hand. She stopped at the barrier and tapped it against an upright metal pole containing some electromagnetic wizardry.

The security barrier shot up by 90 degrees, allowing me to proceed forward. That white plastic card would be the key to opening all future doors and services, and it was so important that the campsite levied a 30 euro deposit for its safe return.

We had been assigned a grassy pitch numbered 29. It was at the top of a steep incline overlooking the campsite. We were the only camper in this touring designated area, and the grassy pitch was anything but grassy. The Grand Duchy of Luxembourg must have been subjected to torrential rain over the preceding few days, as our designated number 29 was full of puddles and very muddy. I checked out the neighbouring pitches and found one, numbered 32, that was slightly less muddy. I noted the number and marched down the steep incline to the reception area. "To march down" was an appropriate idiom as the place felt very regimented and ordered, akin to a military compound.

At reception, I explained that our designated command post was too muddy and warned that our personnel carrier might get bogged down in trench sludge. I then referenced the other, slightly less slushy pitch and requested an immediate strategic withdrawal to this more advantageous position.

Not a single word was spoken by the receptionist. The white magnetic card was taken from my hand, scanned, and then, after a few computer clicks, returned with an approving nod. I left the mute receptionist and returned to the camper. As soon as we had relocated to pitch number 32 and hooked up to the mains, we settled down for the remainder of the afternoon. It had been a long drive from Ancona, and the three of us needed a rest from the driving.

Somewhere between Chambéry and Luxembourg, I managed to post a quick update to our travel blog.

I included a photo of Vangelis that I had photo-shopped onto a stock image of the Colosseum in Rome and another of him in front of the Eiffel Tower in Paris. I gave my update the title:

"Postcards from Vangelis - To his worldwide fan club" and wrote the following:

We are currently somewhere in France. The Channel coast is still a distance away, and so is the final hurdle of Vangelis's journey: The UK authorities.

We had his EU pet passport checked by a second vet in Greece, and he has received all his shots and meds. As far as we are concerned, we have ticked all the boxes and done all we can to ensure he passes all the regulations and gets through UK pet controls.

We have never travelled across a controlled border with a pet before, and we've come too far for this to go wrong. So, guys and girls! To all of you who have followed this remarkable story of a kitten who has survived hunger, dehydration, and wildfires. And to all of you who have posted such heartfelt and amazing comments over the past three months, from Western Canada to China, South Africa to Australia and New Zealand, the USA, and across Europe and beyond. If you have a charm, a prayer, a talisman, or some kind of "juju," now is the time to make that call. Keep everything crossed, and send Vangelis your positive vibes and love for a happy ending to this latest chapter.

When I checked my blog post in Luxembourg, it had reached nearly 50,000, received almost 600 reactions, and garnered over 150 heartwarming comments:

"Fingers and toes crossed for this little legend!"

"Rooting for Vangelis. Good luck, guys, and keep us posted."

"I love Vangelis and pray for his safe arrival in the UK. Please keep on letting us know about that beautiful boy's progress."

"Love you, Vangelis, and prayers for safe passage."

"A heartwarming story. It's great to read something positive. Thanks."

Vangelis may have had one last hurdle before entering the UK .... but so did we. COVID restrictions and regulations were still very much in effect, and Eurotunnel required every passenger to have a negative PCR test result before travelling on the shuttle.

I checked online and found a screening centre in Arras, northern France. It was about a four-hour drive away and was open every day except Sundays. There was also a huge camper stop in Arras with all the facilities. Perfect!

So, the following day, Friday, we packed up and vacated our muddy pitch. To exit the campground, Claire had to tap the white card against the upright metal pole, which again interacted magically with the electromagnetic wizardry within, and the barrier flew open. I advanced a few metres, parked, and waited for Claire, who had returned to reception to claim our 30 euro deposit.

We reached Arras, and its fantastic camper stop, early in the afternoon and parked near a grassy area where Vangelis could play out. The plan was to walk into the town centre the following morning, find the screening centre, and get tested.

Results were usually emailed within a few hours, so we'd have time to upload them well before our shuttle service on Sunday afternoon. We also had to complete an online Passenger Locator Form (PLF) for the UK authorities. This was a little tricky because our unvaccinated status meant that we would have to self-isolate for 10 days on arrival. However, as non-UK residents, we figured that transiting to the Isle of Man would exempt us from this requirement.

In the section *"Are you required to self-isolate in the UK?"* we wrote *"No"* and then proceeded to tick the box *"Transiting landside in the UK, departing through England only"* and *"Testing exemption declared."* Evidence of onward travel also had to be provided.

We uploaded the PLF and heard nothing back. Presumably, had there been any issues, we would have been contacted prior to leaving France. Satisfied that our UK PLF had been submitted correctly, the only other task at hand was the PCR tests.

On Saturday morning, we strolled into the centre of Arras without a care in the world. The sun was shining brightly, and the streets were surprisingly busy with many blue masked shoppers. It was about as normal as it could be under the circumstances. The address for the screening centre led us to a large pharmacy similar to a British high street *Boots* store.

Inside were aisles dedicated to Beauty and Skincare, Fragrance, Baby and Child, Wellness and Toiletries. We couldn't see a sign for PCR tests, so I approached the busy pharmacy dispensing counter next to the *Click and Collect* and asked a masked assistant. I couldn't see her facial expression because her face was covered, but her eyes narrowed with uncertainty as she turned to a male colleague. He stepped forward and asked me what I wanted.

When I explained that we needed a PCR test, his eyes widened as he glanced at his wristwatch. His chest puffed up, and he exhaled so forcefully that his mask bulged slightly outwards.

It was about twenty minutes to midday, and the pharmacy's screening service was only available between 09:00 and 12:00 on Saturdays! Also, this was the only clinic in Arras that provided the test facility. We were unaware of any of this, and after explaining our travel requirements and predicament to the pharmacist, he agreed to rush through a test for us.

We followed him down a narrow corridor to a small room, where he excused himself momentarily. A few minutes later, he reappeared fully clad in personal protective equipment (PPE). This guy was taking his role very seriously. He had a blue scrub cap on his head, a full knee-length gown, gloves, and a mask, all topped off with a flimsy plastic visor, just to be on the safe side.

I dutifully arched my head back while he swabbed the back of my nostrils, popping the nasopharyngeal swabbing stick into a sealable plastic tube afterwards. Once Claire had been swabbed, we had to return to the counter and pay 30 euros each at check-out. Unbeknownst to us, the French government terminated its free COVID testing policy in mid-summer in favour of profitability.

The pharmacist told us the test results would be emailed later that day and wished us a *"Bon Voyage."* We shuffled outside into the sunshine, feeling somewhat ripped off by the whole affair. If governments insist on citizens getting tested, then they should be free of charge!

When we returned to the camper, Vangelis was itching to get outside for his afternoon leg stretch and sniff-about. It hadn't been much fun for him in Luxembourg, where, despite our best efforts, he'd managed to get covered right up to his ears in mud. At least, in Arras, the camper stop had adequate drainage, and the afternoon sunshine had dried up the grassy ground behind us.

It was our last night on the mainland of Europe and, for us, the last night of the trip. Over the next 48 hours, we'd be in transit back to the Isle of Man, where we would have to adhere to yet another set of COVID rules and protocols.

Calais is only an hour's drive from Arras, and our shuttle was scheduled for 4:22 p.m. Nevertheless, we intended to allow all three of us plenty of time for check-in and passport formalities. So, after a coffee or two on Sunday morning, we packed up, topped up with fresh water, and got on the road for Calais. With a few stops for shopping, gas, and diesel, we reached the Eurotunnel terminal around lunchtime and drove straight to the Pet Reception carpark.

The red pet carrier box Yana had given us proved its worth once again. With his passport and travel documents in hand, we placed Vangelis inside the box and walked over to the reception building.

A British couple was ahead of us with two large Golden Labrador dogs. As we waited in line, the conversation between the couple and the receptionist became increasingly tense and edgy. There was an issue with the dog's UK animal health certificates. The young French receptionist calmly pointed out that the dog's documents did not indicate recent treatment for tapeworm. She tried to explain that UK authorities require tapeworm treatment to be administered by a vet not less than 24 hours and no more than five days before the scheduled arrival time in the UK. None of this had been done, and the couple, finally, had to turn around and leave with their two dogs in tow. On a Sunday afternoon in Calais, finding a vet at such short notice would probably have been difficult for them. Then, it was our turn to get Vangelis checked.

I handed the pet passport to the receptionist, who, in turn, gave me a microchip scanner. I was instructed to pass the scanner over his body where the chip had been inserted. As soon as the carrier's hatch opened, Vangelis attempted to get out, but we stopped him in time and quickly passed the scanner over his left shoulder. It beeped once and displayed a long 15-digit number. The receptionist checked this against the numbered barcode in the passport, nodded approvingly, and then proceeded to flick through the pages until she reached the rabies vaccination status. So far, so good!

Then she flicked through the passport, from cover to cover, several times searching for *something.* It was excruciating for us because, with each page turn, her eyebrows furrowed even more. Whatever she was searching for was missing, and the silence was becoming intense.

"Where is the entry for tapeworm treatment?" she asked, dangling the passport between her finger and thumb. I felt the carotid artery on my neck's left side flex with an

involuntary spasm. *"He doesn't require any worm treatment,"* I murmured. *"He is a cat!" "Oh, it's a cat!"* she chuckled, and at that precise moment, Vangelis made his presence known with a loud outburst.

I pointed to the red box and again confirmed that the loud meow belonged to a cat. A cat that, according to the UK Government's DEFRA website, did not need to be treated for tapeworms, roundworms, hookworms, or any kind of worms prior to entry into the UK. She apologised for the faux pas and returned Vangelis's passport and a paper pass to display from inside the windscreen.

Outside, we hugged each other, Claire cried with joy, and Vangelis remained oblivious to the whole affair, apart from a croaky grumble. The sheer relief at getting him one step closer to home was indescribable. All that apprehension, concern, worry, and irrational anxiety we had put ourselves through vanished into thin air. We were jumping for joy!

Next, it was our turn to check-in for the shuttle and pass through passport controls. We pulled up alongside one of the manned check-in booths at about 1:00 p.m., three hours ahead of our scheduled departure time. As had happened in 2020, the assistant offered us an earlier slot, which we gratefully accepted. This free-of-charge change in plan meant we would arrive almost three hours earlier in England.

After clearing the French and UK border controls, we followed instructions to park behind a lane of waiting vehicles. About 20 minutes later, we were directed down a ramp and onto the waiting shuttle. With all vehicles loaded and secured, the shuttle began its 35-minute, 88 mph journey under the English Channel.

As it trundled along at a depth of 75 metres below sea level, we could hardly believe how quickly and efficiently the entire procedure had been completed.

Following on from the legal obligations of travelling across borders with a pet and the uncertainties they had created for us, I reminded myself of the famous quote by Dale Carnegie:

"Today is the tomorrow you worried about yesterday."

I also couldn't wait to write about our achievement and publish the latest update to the Rocking Life on the Road travel blog page. I knew thousands of Vangelis's fans and followers would eagerly anticipate this happy outcome.

On arrival in Folkstone, there were no checks or inspections of the Passenger Locator Forms or our exemptions from the 10-day self-isolation period.

So we joined the M20 motorway north to the M25 and continued until we reached the Midlands. We'd be travelling for at least nine hours since leaving Arras and decided to rest for the night at a truck stop near Walsall. It was hardly the most glamorous location, after all the beautiful places we'd visited, but it felt safe and secure and was within walking distance of a pub still serving grub!

Before bed, I tapped out a post for our travel page. Photos of Vangelis outside the pet reception centre and inside the shuttle on his way to the UK were included, and I titled the post:

"Vangelis has arrived in the British Isles. Hooray!"

Along with full details of the day's events, I also summarised the entire story of one little, lost kitten's journey from a beach in Greece all the way across Europe to the British Isles. I ended the post with the following words:

Tonight, we are all winners and very, very happy!
Thank you, everyone, for your best wishes, prayers and
We really appreciate it all.
Love Vangelis, Derek & Claire xxxxx

I clicked "post" and hit the sack.

The following morning, we were amazed that the post had already reached thousands of people and received hundreds of reactions and responses worldwide. Overall, there was a genuine sense of relief and joy from the many heartfelt comments:

"My eyes are all blurry after reading this! OMG, that's amazing!"

"Wonderful news. I think the British Government may have had a world uprising on their hands had they not allowed Vangelis in!"

"Fate is an amazing thing. You were all supposed to meet that evening."

"This is so lovely to hear. Vangelis is a legend already."

"Tears of joy are running down my cheeks for you all. I can't tell you how happy I am that you have all arrived safely in the UK."

"So, so happy, amazing, brilliant news! You should write a book about this journey!"

Before we could travel home to the Isle of Man, we had to complete an Isle of Man Government online COVID landing form and declare our vaccination status. Claire had submitted this form for both of us the day before, and a response was emailed back that morning. We were each given a landing card reference number, a QR code to present on arrival, along with our photographic ID, and a choice of two options.

Under the *Direction Notice* attached to the email, we had to either isolate for 21 days from the date of arrival or opt for a PCR test and isolate for six days. This second option, called the *6-Day Pathway*, cost £30 per person. When filling out the online landing form, we had already selected the 6-day isolation option and booked the obligatory PCR test.

With only 130 miles remaining until we reached the ferry terminal in Heysham, we set off from our truck stop near Walsall in the pouring rain for this last leg of the trip.

For the three-and-a-half-hour sea crossing, we decided to leave Vangelis in the camper. He'd found his sea legs, after all, on the long sailing from Greece to Italy, and staying in the camper was a much more comfortable option for him.

The ferry was on time, and we reached Douglas just after 6:15 p.m. The disembarking traffic was directed to a terminal carpark where health officials screened all passengers. After scanning our QR codes, we were told to drive directly to our home, stay there until the following morning, and then drive to the designated test centre for PCR swabbing. It was like a military operation with many officials on hand, sporting high-visibility security vests and directing the traffic.

After clearing COVID security, we were on our way and could hardly wait to introduce Vangelis to his forever home. It was dark and still pouring rain when we manoeuvred the camper into the small drive in front of our house. Claire grabbed the red box with Vangelis inside while I ran ahead to open the front door. We placed the box inside the hallway on the floor and opened the hatch.

Moments later, he slowly crawled out, stretched his back legs, sniffed the floor, and swaggered slowly towards the living room as if he owned the place. He shook his paws vigorously with each step as if he'd just stepped in water or glue. *"It's the carpet!"* Claire laughed. *"It's the first time he has ever walked on carpet, and he's not sure what it is."*

The laminate floors elsewhere in the house were like skating rinks, only because he zoomed around at full gallop for the first couple of hours. The washing machine had him bewildered, and he just sat in front of it, turning his head in circles as the suds whirled around.

The TV was another mystery, and he kept checking behind it, wondering where the *other people* had gone. The stairs also amused him, and he spent ages just running up and down them, occasionally leaping from the top of the stairs down onto the landing below before repeating the same stunt over and over. Our wood-burning stove in the living room initially made him very wary, but he soon understood that it was a wonderful source of warmth and comfort.

Ours was the first house he had ever been in, so everything was a mystery and an exciting new adventure.

It's probably fair to say that, within the first 24 hours, he became familiar with every room, nook, and cranny in the house. He also settled in almost immediately and established himself as the King of the Castle.

As for us? Well, we were over the moon! We'd done it. We'd ticked all the boxes and covered the miles to ensure our little *Messenger of Good News* came back home with us.

Since that fateful evening, three months earlier, on a small deserted beach in Evia, he had travelled over 3,400 miles with us across Greece, Italy, France, Luxembourg, and the UK to reach the Isle of Man. And along the way, he'd become a superstar! Wooing, charming, and cheering many thousands of folks worldwide with his antics, high jinks, and adventures.

In the days following our release from isolation, a local media group contacted us. Vangelis's fame and good fortune had preceded him to the Isle of Man, and a reporter from the newspaper *Manx Independent* wanted the full scoop. An interview was scheduled, and a photographer was sent to take photos. We chose the location for the photoshoot—a small, picturesque sandy beach called Gansey Bay, not far from home. After all, a beach seemed the perfect location, all things considered.

Vangelis's article appeared in the newspaper's November 4th, 2021 edition under the heading:

"Kitten's fame after rescue from wildfires" and was given a full-page spread.

3FM, a local radio station also contacted me for an exclusive on the Isle of Man's latest celebrity resident. Vangelis was also featured in a local *Pet of the Week* competition and won second prize to a cockerel! He was invited into the studio at *3FM radio* and presented with a large goodies hamper and a comfy bed.

During the weeks and months following our return home, we'd be stopped in unlikely places like the bank, a furniture store, the local recycling centre, etc., and asked, *"How's the cat?"*

Meanwhile, the online interest surrounding Vangelis hadn't abated for a single moment, and I was still kept busy writing regular updates to our Rocking Life on the Road travel page. Every post garnered the same positive and enthusiastic reactions and commentary:

"Can't wait to read the news article. Vangelis is a superstar and is loved all around the world!"

"Thank you for keeping us fans updated."

"Bright lights of Hollywood beckoning!"

"Vangelis is such a celebrity."

"He's landed on his four paws."

"His story deserves to be told."

****

Epilogue - Επίλογος

(Greek Word!)

The adventures of Vangelis introduced us to so many new friends and acquaintances, both online and in person, from all across the world.

We could never have imagined the outcome, the day we left the beach in Evia with that scrawny little kitten asleep on Claire's lap.

Our travels across Greece and our return home to the Isle of Man generated a constant stream of compassion, kind-heartedness, goodwill, and positivity.

All this happened during the COVID-19 pandemic, a period of significant global disruption that subjected people worldwide to isolation, loneliness, worries, financial difficulties, and mental health problems, not to mention the fear of catching the virus.

Since 2021, Vangelis has travelled on every trip we've been on. In fact, since that year, he has travelled over 30,000 miles with us, visiting the following 22 European countries:

Albania
Austria
Belgium
Bosnia-Herzegovina
Bulgaria
Croatia
Czech Republic
England
France

Germany
Greece
Hungary
Ireland
Italy
Luxembourg
Montenegro
Poland
Romania
Scotland
Serbia
Slovakia
The Netherlands

In 2022, we returned to Evia and parked at the exact location where Vangelis had found us. One afternoon, while I was cooling off in the sea, a lady stopped by to pat and pamper the famous kitty lounging in the shade. I swam back to shore and went to say hello. The lady was from Athens and on holiday with her husband and another couple. She smiled at me and said assuredly, *"You were here last year."* Her words puzzled me because we hadn't met or spoken to anyone during our short stay.

She continued, *"I remember your face and this camper. My husband was very inquisitive about the registration number."* She also recalled seeing something else scurrying about in between our feet. *"Is this the kitten we saw you with last year?"*

She then invited us to join her group on the beach for the rest of the afternoon. It was the beginning of a wonderful and enduring friendship, and we've kept in close contact with the lovely Maria, her husband

Michaelis, and their friends Billy and Christína ever since.

In July 2023, we met again with Maria and Michaelis on *Vangelis's beach.* There was another reunion with all four of our Greek friends the following summer.

Another big surprise occurred during our annual pilgrimage to Evia in 2024. A retired couple, Anna and Yianni, who own a small cottage nearby, invited me to pick lemons from their orchard. At their home, I was told a story that left me dumbfounded.

Anna spoke of a cat that had given birth to a litter of kittens near an adjacent property. The month and year was July 2021, shortly before wildfires broke out and devasted the island's north. She also spoke of a hungry fox that had been stalking the area, searching for a free lunch. As a consequence of this predator, the mother cat had started moving her litter, kitten by kitten, to a safer location. During this kitty evacuation, three escaped from the nest and wandered off. Anna described how one kitten disappeared into the long grass and was never seen again while another played and clung to her sandal. *"She was like a little dancer at the end of my foot,"* Anna said, *"so I named her Carla after the famous Italian prima ballerina Carla Fracci."*

"And the third kitten?" I asked. Anna smiled and explained that it had continued down the beach road towards a lone camper van parked about 200 metres further along.

Anna kept Carla safe at the cottage until she could be rehomed. She now lives in Athens with her son and his family.

****

I have thoroughly enjoyed writing this account of our travels during 2020-21 and, of course, the star of the show himself, the *Messenger of Good News*, Vangelis. This book would never have seen the light of day had we not made that left turn at the last moment, down a single-track road lined with olive trees, looking for a place to park for the night. Did this happen for a reason? Was it meant to be? Was it all just a coincidence?

Maybe Yana had the answer when she said:

"Animals have a purpose when they come into our lives."

"Τα ζώα έχουν ένα σκοπό όταν μπαίνουν στη ζωή μας."

****

Follow Derek & Claire
and the Adventures of
Vangelis:

www.facebook.com/rockinglifeontheroad

www.instagram.com/rockinglifeontheroad

Derek's Drone Videos:

www.youtube.com/@dronescape9991

Claire's Crochet:

"Fuglylove Creations" on Facebook

Contact: dallen@manx.net

****

Printed in Great Britain
by Amazon